The Secret Lives of Booksellers and Librarians

The Secret Lives *of* Booksellers *and* Librarians

TRUE STORIES *of the* MAGIC *of* READING

JAMES PATTERSON

and MATT EVERSMANN

with CHRIS MOONEY

Little, Brown and Company
New York Boston London

Little, Brown and Company
Hachette Book Group
1290 Avenue of the Americas, New York, NY 10104
littlebrown.com

First Edition: April 2024

Little, Brown and Company is a division of Hachette Book Group, Inc. The Little, Brown name and logo are trademarks of Hachette Book Group, Inc.

The publisher is not responsible for websites (or their content) that are not owned by the publisher.

The Hachette Speakers Bureau provides a wide range of authors for speaking events. To find out more, go to hachettespeakersbureau .com or email hachettespeakers@hbgusa.com.

Little, Brown and Company books may be purchased in bulk for business, educational, or promotional use. For information, please contact your local bookseller or the Hachette Book Group Special Markets Department at special.markets@hbgusa.com.

ISBN 9780316567534 (hardcover) / 9780316572828 (large print) / 9780316577915 (signed edition) / 9780316577908 (B&N signed edition)
LCCN 2023937340

Printing 1, 2024

LSC-C

Printed in the United States of America

CONTENTS

Author's Note
vii

PART ONE
To be a bookseller, you have to play detective.
1

PART TWO
I could talk about books forever.
71

PART THREE
I can't imagine what people do without books in their lives.
141

PART FOUR
It doesn't matter what you like to read, as long as you love to read.
213

PART FIVE
Just one more chapter, please, just one more chapter.
279

AUTHOR'S NOTE

You are holding a book in your hands right now. Or maybe listening to one. If you live in America, you're among only one in five who *can* read a book and are actually *in the habit* of reading books. To my way of thinking, that statistic is dystopian.

In America we urge everyone over the age of eighteen to vote, but only 15 percent of voters read books. Only 15 percent of us perform the life-affirming, sanity-bolstering, empathy-forming act of spending time inside somebody else's brain.

Fortunately—in spite of cell phones, in spite of video games, in spite of online gambling and porn, in spite of the current storm of shortsighted politics—the habit of reading books is not yet on the brink of extinction.

Not yet.

This is in no small part due to an elite corps of frontline workers, people who are holding that line, and sometimes even turning the tide. I'm talking about the thousands of booksellers and librarians working long hours to keep reading alive and getting little recognition for all that they do.

Today's booksellers and librarians are not the sitcom stereotypes who give judgy looks when someone brings the latest bestseller to the counter, or who will *shush* an overenthusiastic teen to churchy quiet from sixty yards away.

Today's booksellers and librarians are extraordinarily good at understanding and motivating. Armed with empathy, wit, and professional training, they take the confused, the fearful, the frustrated, and help them become more keen-eyed, sharp-eared, and justice-attuned. What they do is crucial for this country, especially right now. They understand in their hearts and souls that *in the beginning was the word.*

Day after day after day, they find the right book for the right person, and in so doing, they help save people's—and our collective—lives. And maybe our sanity.

To my mind, there are no professions more noble than bookseller and librarian.

Nor, as you will soon read, are there professionals who are more surprising and inspiring.

—James Patterson

PART ONE

To be a bookseller,
you have to play detective.

Alexis Sky

Alexis Sky lives outside Albany, New York, and has two bookselling homes: the Book House of Stuyvesant Plaza in Albany and Market Block Books in downtown Troy, New York.

Ah, I just love that smell," I hear a customer say to a friend as I'm doing some shelving at the back of the bookstore.

"What smell?" his friend says.

"The smell of a bookstore," the first customer replies. "It smells like books in here!"

I chuckle, but I know exactly what he means. Most chain stores either open into a mall, or they smell like coffee—or both. But walk into an independent bookshop, and there's a particular intoxicating book scent.

It's definitely not available online.

I head to the front to grab a box of books, and the customer spots me.

"Excuse me," he says, holding up his phone. "I need this book."

"What book are you talking about?"

"This one, from the interview this woman just posted." He turns to his friend, saying, "I don't know who does their social media, but it's on point."

I peer at the customer's phone. "That's just me!"

We both laugh.

This is a small independent shop. We don't have a store manager. I do returns. I do the buying. I do the receiving. I run the website. And I do all the social media, which I absolutely love, even if I'm not the typical demographic. I mean, my first Facebook account was in college, when it was still called The Facebook.

I find the book and hand it to him. "Here it is. It's really good."

"I know. I watched your video," he says. "I had five of my friends follow you because I love your recommendations. You do a great eclectic mix."

This is why I love my job. My heart's plugged into this work.

A lot of customers tell me they feel the same way. *Hey, who's this Alexis person? I like all the books she's recommended. What else is she suggesting?*

I love witnessing the excitement kids feel, walking out the door hugging their books. Or overhearing adults say, "It's been so long since I picked up a book, but, man, I couldn't put this one down. I read it until one in the morning."

To me, books are the greatest kind of escapism. I may have a master's degree, but one of my favorite books is *Twilight*. It's just escapist fiction at its absolute best. To each their own, but my attitude is: *Listen, I have a kid at home, I have a full-time job. I teach. I have a big life. But I don't want to think about my big life for a little while.* For two hours, I am not Alexis in Albany. I am in the world of Forks, or I am in Wonderland, or I am in Hogwarts.

One time a girl comes in, and I suggest a favorite book of mine. (The author claims my personal recommendations are the reason it's still in print.) "It's a beautiful book," I tell the girl. "Please try it."

A week later, she's back in the store looking for me. It's my day off, but she doesn't want anyone else's help. The next time I'm scheduled to work, she's waiting at the door.

"Okay, it's been two days. What else do you recommend? I need at least three books."

Some customers I even buy for outright—I put books I know they'll like on the hold shelf. I have one older woman customer who loves racy romance novels, and now for every holiday her husband comes in to buy her gift certificates and ask if I've set anything aside.

When I hand him a stack of books, he smiles and says, "This is why you shop independent."

There is nothing better than that phrase. That's all I need to hear.

I live in Watervliet, outside of Albany, New York, but I grew up west of here in a tiny little town with an amazing library and local independent bookstore, Mysteries on Main Street. I've been an indie girl since I was old enough to spend my weekly allowance on books—not that my allowance even covered what I bought, but the bookseller just could not say no to me. I swear my dad must've had to go down regularly to pay my tab.

It's not as if we had a huge disposable income. I was the oldest of five. My mom was a payroll accountant at a local mill, and my dad owns a stained-glass business.

But my parents are voracious readers too. My mom is the head coordinator of our local Jane Austen Society. So my parents always made sure I had a huge bookcase in my room, and they had an arrangement with our local librarians: I was allowed to borrow any book, as long as they were kept informed.

"Alexis is reading an adult book today. You might want to have a discussion." That was the extent of it. No one forbade anything.

Often, those adult books went right over my head anyway. One of my dad's favorite stories is how once, when I was eight years old, I looked up from my book and asked him, "Daddy, what's ether?"

"I'm sorry, what?" he replied, a little confused. "What are you reading about? Animals or science or something?"

"Oh no, I read about it in this awesome book," I told him.

"It's about these two best friends who go to this mythical land called Las Vegas. They go to a casino, and to a circus that gives them money. And, Daddy, they ride these things called dune buggies. I don't know what it is, but I want one."

"Oh my God," my dad said. "You're reading *Fear and Loathing in Las Vegas*?"

"It's like *Alice in Wonderland* for boys, right?"

My dad grasped the lifeline I threw and said, "Yes, Alexis. That's exactly what *Fear and Loathing in Las Vegas* is about. It's about two best friends who go to Wonderland. Yes. And when you turn eighteen, please reread the book and we'll have a different conversation."

My first job after getting my master's degree in art history and museum studies is at a museum, but they just don't have the hours. So when I notice that Borders, the big book chain at the mall, is looking for workers, I go in to apply.

"We're only hiring for cash register," Gary, the assistant manager, tells me. "But if you prove yourself, I'll put you on the red table."

A lot of the kids who work at the store are just there to ring out a register. They don't read. They're not there for the books. They're literally there because it's a better job than working fast food, and I don't blame them. It is a dang good job.

But the red table turns out to be where all the people like me go. We all have master's degrees in subjects like philosophy or women's studies, and we're all working here because we love books. Borders is a big corporation, but Gary has an independent-bookstore mindset. "I want people who read. I want people who are interested. I want dynamic voices on the floor. I want diverse people on the floor."

I'm there for about a year and a half when I'm asked if I want a management position. Then, the very next day, we find out that Borders has declared bankruptcy and all the stores will be closing.

"Well, we still want you to be a manager."

Of what, a sinking ship?

"You know furniture, you used to work in a museum. You can be in charge of selling all the furniture," I'm told.

The furniture? I know mahogany. I know Stickley. "I'm not selling books anymore? I just sell furniture?"

Exactly.

Well, guess what? I *do* sell all the furniture. No other Borders store can say that. No other store has every piece of their furniture gone. I even get a bonus.

One of the people I sell to is Susan Novotny. Susan owns the Book House, a 6,000-square-foot independent bookstore in Stuyvesant Plaza, a huge open-air shopping center in Albany. She also owns the Little Book House, the children's bookstore next to the Book House, and Market Block Books, a smaller, more elegant and curated bookshop, in nearby Troy.

"I love the Book House," I tell Susan as I load her up with racks and book carts.

Later I find out that Susan went to Gary and asked, "If there was one person that you would suggest to the Book House for a full-time position, somebody who's flexible, somebody who's a hard worker, who would you pick?"

"Alexis, without a doubt," he tells her. "If you can scoop that girl up, do it."

When Susan comes back to me with a job offer, I accept immediately. "What day do you close?" she asks.

"Thursday," I tell her.

"Can you start on Friday?" she asks.

That was eleven years ago. She scooped me right up and it's just been incredible.

We all really do feel like a family at the Book House and Market Block Books. My daughter, Molly, is called the Bookstore Baby, since she's grown up in the stacks. There's nothing the other staff and I wouldn't do to help out Susan and the stores.

The way the public rallies when coronavirus hits really touches me. Susan is confident from the start. She pulls me aside early on and says, "I think they're going to shut us down. But don't worry. The business will survive this. Our community will ensure it. We will ensure it."

And damn, did we. Susan fights for us to be allowed to fill orders and do deliveries. "We should be open. We are bookstores. We are pillars of the community."

With the libraries closed, she works with a couple of programs to get books delivered to children. So while food is being delivered by the Boys and Girls Club, so are books. Nourishment for their brains.

One day during lockdown, a man comes up and starts banging on the bookshop door. "I'm so sorry, sir," I tell him through the glass. "I can't open the door for you."

He slaps a piece of paper on the window. It's a check for $400. "This is for kids. This is for their books. Please buy them books."

I start crying. "Oh my God. You have no idea what this means. I've met some of the children who need these books. Thank you."

"That was from my company." Then he pulls out another $100 and says, "And this is personally from me. Tell Susan, goddamn, thank you, thank you."

The generosity of the community blows me away, because everyone is struggling yet people keep coming by, asking, "How many books can I buy for these kids? What can we do?" After a while it changes to "How do we support you now? How do we make sure you stay open?"

Stay here. Shop with us. Stay local. Not just at our store but at all these other stores. We're all trying to survive. We're here as a part of your community because you're *our* community.

Lorrie Roussin

*Lorrie Roussin is a librarian at Luna Middle
School in San Antonio, Texas.*

What's that you're reading? Is it any good?"

I look up to see one of the other eighth graders stand-ing at the bus stop. I've been totally absorbed in my book, *The Voice of the Clown* by Brenda Brown Canary, a pulp horror paperback novel with a lurid cover.

I'm a military brat, and my family has just come back to Texas after three years living in England. England is where I discovered my latest favorite authors, Agatha Christie and Sir Arthur Conan Doyle—I consumed those books like crazy, checking out six or seven at a time from the library. I lived and breathed them. I'd get in trouble for bringing books to the family dinner table. I wouldn't even put them down to sleep. At midnight or two a.m., I'd still be telling my parents, "One more chapter."

Even if, as a ten- or eleven-year-old, I might've missed the nuances, I still thought they were fascinating.

The Voice of the Clown isn't on the same level, but I talk it up to a classmate, describing the plot about a little girl and her creepy clown doll, and I hint at some jaw-dropping scenes.

All the other kids at the bus stop are also hooked. They beg to borrow the book from me.

"Okay, but one at a time," I tell them. I start a checkout list, just like in the library. The paperback book gets passed from kid to kid—it's so popular, I eventually have to put Con-Tact paper on the cover to protect it.

I'm thrilled to share what I'm reading with other people.

I'm a natural-born librarian.

At first, though, I go into teaching. Given my love of literature, I figure that being an English teacher makes the most sense, but soon I realize that my real passion is being a school librarian. In Texas, school librarians need a master's degree and two years of teaching experience—and I do enjoy teaching. But now I get to focus on books, and on teaching what I love.

I've been a school librarian for twenty-six years now, in elementary, middle, and high schools. Middle school is where I feel I really belong.

High school kids are so busy—with their AP classes, their part-time jobs, their sports schedules. But middle schoolers still have time to talk to me about books. They're curious. They have more time to read. And they still want to be read to out loud.

The whole genre of young adult didn't really exist when I was their age. There were basically children's books and adult books, and not much in between except maybe Beverly Cleary, Nancy Drew or the Hardy Boys, and Judy Blume. I read everything Judy Blume wrote—even *Forever,* though that one was in the adult section, so I had to get my parents' permission.

Once I outgrew children's books, though, I pretty much just transitioned right into books like *Jaws, The Exorcist, The Amityville Horror.* Or Jackie Collins novels. I remember being with my mother, in line at the grocery store, and picking up Jackie Collins's latest romance, *Hollywood Husbands,* a lusty story of high-powered fame and fortune.

"Are you sure you want that?" my mother asked, skeptical.

"Oh, Mom, I already read the first one, *Hollywood Wives,*" I scoffed.

Now it's a whole different world. There's an entire young adult arm of the American Library Association (YALSA, the Young Adult Library Services Association), with their own reading lists and book awards. I'm on some of their reading committees, and we're always on the lookout for books that are well written, that draw in reluctant readers, that have representation, that will appeal to a wide audience. I also help choose titles for the Texas Library Association's Texas Maverick Graphic Novels Reading List (TMGNRL) for middle and high schoolers.

I never feel reading burnout because young adult has so many different genres to choose from. And I'm a fan of audiobooks and ebooks too. I'm always reading two or three books, either on my phone or the iPad I carry in my bag. I listen to audiobooks while I'm taking a walk around the lake and playing *Pokémon Go*. Even if I'm in line for the roller coaster at Six Flags Fiesta Texas, I'm reading.

My students call me a walking book blog. All they have to do is come in and say, "Hey, I'm looking for this, this, and this," and I'll find them a dozen books to consider. I always give them freedom of choice. It's okay not to want to read certain books, or not to like certain books.

Encouraging kids to read gives them tools to safely navigate the real world, and to protect themselves. Reading helps them think critically—and it gives them the opportunity to learn about themselves and others, to create empathy and compassion. Students need to be able to see themselves in books, but also to be exposed to and experience somebody else's life through books. Books are supposed to trigger conversations. So when we get book challenges, people saying, "We don't want our kids reading a certain type of book," it makes things really hard.

No one needs to be attacked for differences of opinion.

But any discussions should be done in a respectful manner. I mean, that's what books are supposed to do. We may not agree on certain things, but we can agree to disagree, and this is how we do it. And then you learn things, because there are nuances that you can pick apart and talk about.

I don't know why some adults don't think that kids are capable of understanding or making decisions for themselves. Trust me, these students will tell you what they like and what they want and what they need.

"Ms. Roussin! Ms. Roussin, Ms. Roussin, come here!"

The student storms into the library, calling for me at the top of her lungs. "Ms. Roussin, you've got to come here!"

What did I do? This is the same girl who came to me a few days ago, reluctantly looking for a book to read for class. I'd handed her *All American Boys* by Jason Reynolds and Brendan Kiely.

She stands in front of me, still worked up. "Ms. Roussin, this is the first book I've read that had *me* in it." It just blew her away.

The same thing happens with another student. Over the Thanksgiving break, he takes home a stack of books, including *All American Boys*.

"Ms. Roussin," he declares when he returns, "I read this book. Then my brother read this book. And then my mother read this book. And then my *grandmother* read this book. And now she says she's going to buy me all of this author's books."

There's no better feeling than knowing I helped make this connection, not only for my student, but for his entire family.

Judy Blume

Judy Blume is a renowned author of books for children and adults, and, with her husband, George Cooper, founded and runs Books & Books @ The Studios of Key West in Key West, Florida.

Different books speak to us at different times. I am now eighty-four. So I was seventy-eight when we started the store.

I had decided after fifty years—fifty *years* of writing—that I didn't want to write anymore. It wasn't because the stories weren't there. Stories are always there. I just didn't want to sit in a room all by myself and spend another five years, assuming I had another five years, writing another long book.

I just didn't want to do it anymore.

As a writer, going into a bookstore, you have no idea what really goes on there. You're treated like a queen, and you do what you do, and then you leave. You talk, of course, to the people who are in the bookstores, who are always wonderful and friendly. But you really don't know.

When I was growing up in the 1950s, in Elizabeth, New Jersey, department stores still sold books. My mother went to Bamberger's, a store in Newark, to order three books that she'd seen advertised in the newspaper—the start of Maud Hart Lovelace's Betsy-Tacy series about childhood best friends. Those books quickly became my favorites.

I had, by then, read all fourteen books in L. Frank Baum's Oz series. I don't remember where those books came from. I don't remember going shopping for them. In my mind, they were just there in our house. Somebody must have bought them for me. In addition to going to the library every week, the whole family frequented the Ritz Bookshop near my father's dental office in what we called downtown Elizabeth.

In elementary school, maybe junior high school, I remember going by myself to the Ritz to spend my allowance. It was very exciting. I would get a Nancy Drew book, a new one every week. I guess Nancy Drew books were inexpensive then, or perhaps I saved up, because my allowance was maybe a quarter.

What I loved about the Ritz was the way it smelled. I loved walking around touching the books. I'm still doing the same thing seventy years later.

When my husband, George Cooper, and I moved to Key West in 1994, I think there were five local bookstores.

Key West is many things to many people. When we first started coming down here, we would rent a place for three months so I'd have time to finish writing a book. The next year it was six months. And then the question became "What am I going back for? I really like it here."

Ask "What do you love about Key West?" and everybody says the weather. Then they say, "But really it's the people." Key West is a special place with an eclectic group of active people. That's the kind of place it is.

The time came when Key West no longer had any indie bookshops. There we were, with no bookstores aside from one that featured a few new books and mostly remainders. We missed the indie stores.

We'd drive three and a half, four hours, by car, to Miami. Books & Books in Coral Gables is one of our favorite places. Mitchell Kaplan is the owner. He runs a great café on-site, so we would stop for lunch, then shop for books.

Then we'd go back to Key West and George would look for a space that might be good for an indie bookstore. The search went on for several years. He'd say to Mitch, "Come down and look" at this place or that. But the rents were enormously high, so Mitch could not figure out how to get it done.

"If you guys can figure out a way to get a place," Mitch said, "I will be your affiliate. I will help you in every way. I'll be your mentor."

And so when the storefront space came up in the Studios, the new center for the arts in Key West, George suggested a bookstore to the board. "You run it," they said.

We set up as a nonprofit and we don't pay any rent, which is how we can afford to do this. Mitch at Books & Books consults and does our book buying.

It happened so fast, like in a cartoon. We went from wanting an indie bookstore in Key West, to having an indie bookstore in Key West, to running an indie bookstore in Key West.

Before we knew it, one, two, three, Mitch sent a couple of guys, and the shelves were put up, and the tables were brought in. And then cartons of books started arriving.

We didn't know what we were doing. We weren't even set up yet and people were coming in off the street to look in the cartons and say, "I want to buy this. I want to buy that."

One of Mitch's top booksellers came down and gave us a crash course in bookselling. I've never forgotten her advice.

You have to get people excited about books, and excited about buying books. And they are. That's so amazing. You can walk through the gallery into the bookshop and then up the elevator to the wonderful roof garden, where we host events. The view is 360 degrees, the best view in all of Key West. I believe it's a great place.

So the fantasy became reality. The biggest thing that George and I didn't know, that we never imagined—maybe we're just naive—is how much work is involved. Having a store comes with responsibility.

I am not the entrepreneurial person here. George is. He is the business side of Books & Books Key West. I like to think I'm the creative side.

I posted a letter right there on our cash wrap. "Dear book friends, I'm so happy that you're here." And I am so happy that they're there. But I'm not just there to say hello and find books. I'm working. I'm a bookseller.

"Hey, guys," I say to the staff, our teeny-weeny staff, or our volunteers. "We're in business. We have to sell books here. We may be nonprofit, but if we don't sell books, we can't pay our staff and we can't buy the books. So we need to sell the books."

When you have a very small store that carries a lot of titles (7,000), sadly, books have to turn over. Any book that's in print, we can get for you, but when books don't sell, we have to return them. I really hate that, but it's necessary because there are so many new books and there's so little space. You learn that other side, the bookseller's side, because as a writer you never want to return anybody's book.

Our primary customers are tourists, and sometimes repeat tourists. It's not the traditional college spring breakers. It's families and it's people excited about visiting our bookstore. And most of them now know that I'm there.

I sign their books and take pictures with them. I spend a lot of time talking to them and helping them decide which books of mine are right for which kids in their family, or maybe which of the adult books. Some people are surprised and ask, "Oh, you write adult books?"

If somebody says, "Can you recommend a good book?" you have to say to them, "Well, what do you like? What's your latest favorite?" If they've only read mystery, that's great that they love mystery. We have a wonderful section. I show them the table display of new thrillers, then tell them, "Maybe you would also be interested in this other kind of book."

A book I really fell for was a debut novel, *The Paper Palace* by Miranda Cowley Heller. We learned from our sister store in Miami that people really do respond to staff recommendations. But I don't write good staff recs. When people ask me to write blurbs, I'm just no good at it.

But in this case, I wrote a really good staff rec. And we have sold a lot—for us—a lot of copies of this book. Every time it comes in, it sells right out. I noticed yesterday that it was gone again. I know that my best blurb is selling that book.

No one has complained so far. I think, *Oh, somebody's going to come back and say, "I really didn't like that book."* Well, that's okay. That's okay.

I think back to the moment I said, "That's it. Fifty years. I don't want to write anymore." And then this opportunity came up. So how lucky am I, suddenly able to get up in the morning excited about what I'm going to do, how I'm going to spend my day.

I am excited every day that I go to the bookstore. This is the truth.

Sharon Perry Martin

Sharon Perry Martin is library director at the University Park Public Library in University Park, Texas.

If you ever go into a library and you get bad service or no service, just leave.

Librarians often come from all types of careers and walks of life before going to graduate school to get a specialized advanced degree, what used to be called a master's in library science. Now it's library and information science.

No matter the stereotypes about librarians, most of us go into this field because we like to help people. That's what we're here for. We're not doing it for the money or the glory. Though the public's perception is usually a nice one.

"What do you do?" people ask me. "Where do you work?"

"I work in a library," I say. Or "I'm a librarian."

"Oh, that's so nice" is the typical response. "That's wonderful. Thank you for what you do." Or "That must be the best job in the world."

And I will tell you, it *is* the best job in the world.

What I love about libraries is we are the last true bastion of impartiality. If a librarian is trained and if they are doing their job according to American Library Association standards, they serve anyone who walks through the door. We don't keep anybody out of our buildings. And we are impartial. No matter how repugnant or offensive a librarian may find someone's research request or even their reading list, we're trained to help with a straight face and a smile as we hand over the book.

That kind of open exchange is a wonderful thing. Sometimes it happens in reverse.

My first job as an assistant manager is at the Martin Luther King branch in the Dallas Public Library system in South Dallas, Texas. At the time, it's a predominantly African American community, and I am not. I am Caucasian. An elderly gentleman from the community comes in to look at the large African American history collection, but he never asks me for help. He always goes to the circulation desk and asks for the manager, who is from Ghana.

After weeks of this, the manager asks this gentleman why he wouldn't just ask me.

And he says, "Well, she's white, and I don't want to ask anything that might embarrass her or ask her to help me research anything that would make her feel bad."

The manager then convinces him that I am a trained professional and would be glad to help him. After a few more weeks, he begins to let me help him. And we rather enjoy working together.

The gentleman has now passed on, but I remember him for the grace and graciousness that he showed me. It never leaves my heart that he didn't want me to feel uncomfortable working in his community, where he had lived his whole life.

When parents ask me, "What would you let your child read?" I tell them a story.

Many years ago, it was a universal library practice for adults and children to have separate library cards. A child with a children's card could not check out adult books.

I am fourteen or fifteen years old, and my mother drops me off at the library. I want to check out a book about Henry VIII, since my family has recently returned from Europe, where we visited the Tower of London and heard lots of stories about him. When my mother comes to pick me up, she asks me as we're driving home whether I've gotten what I wanted. I tell her that I wasn't allowed to check out an adult book about Henry VIII because I only have a children's card.

My mother is a very quiet person, certainly not outspoken at all. But she whips her car around and U-turns in the middle of downtown Beaumont, Texas, parks in a no-parking zone, and drags me back into the library, where she reads the library staff the riot act for not letting me have that book.

"I'm raising this child," she tells them, "and if I have a problem with something she brings home from the library, she'll hear about it from me. You won't. So you let her have anything she wants."

From that point on, I get an adult card and can check out anything I want. It makes a big impact. So does my mother's taking ownership for raising me, as every parent should. She trusts me not to check out or read books that I'm not supposed to, just the ones that I want to read.

"How can I get more people in to use the library?" That's the question that keeps my brain churning.

At library school, we're not trained to run a business. Yet that's the challenge that every director faces on multiple fronts—from dealing with shrinking budgets to trying to figure out the best way to get more for your money, whether it be with staff or materials. Raising awareness of the library, doing the community outreach and engagement.

I would like a larger percentage of our population in University Park to have library cards and use the library. This is an affluent community, and I'm sure a lot of people buy their own books or ebooks. But we have still not met my goal, which is for 25 percent of our population to have active library cards. We're not there yet. And before I retire, I would like us to get there.

Now that we have self-checkout machines using Radio

Frequency Identification (RFID) technology, some people always use the self-checkout, because they're getting either some sort of fluffy book or a really sexy book that they don't want people to know they're checking out. I work the circulation desk an hour or so a day, and it always makes me laugh to see them putting their hands over the title they do not want the librarians to see.

All the books by a particular racy romance author come back with initials written in pencil in the front of them. I finally figure out that the markings are from a group of elderly ladies, all neighbors and friends. They put their initials in it, pass it on to the next person, but then can't remember whether or not they've read it. So they have to look at their initials to see if they have actually read the book before.

People often get a book title wrong, then are so insistent that they have it right. When I figure out what the patron is really asking for, I have kind of a duh moment.

The one I'll never forget is a customer calling in, looking for *Everything Is Eliminated.* I can't find a book by that title anywhere.

Finally, she turns away from the phone and asks someone else in her household, who tells her that she wants *Everything Is Illuminated* by Jonathan Safran Foer, *F-O-E-R.* What makes me laugh is that, for that book, which eventually became a movie, either title would've worked.

Today there's less room in libraries for print books. I'm not saying they're going away. Libraries are just using a little less space for print books and opening up a lot more functional space: private work areas, collaborative spaces, meeting rooms, study rooms. And of course, we've all increased our digital offerings like crazy. Library patrons can even sign up for a service to watch videos that teach different types of craft skills.

More and more libraries are doing mobile kiosks that can sit in a mall, in a bus station. I've even seen one with a revolving belt that called to mind a sushi place in Japan. Insert your library card and pick the book you want.

People are busy. Why not meet them where they are?

Susan Kehoe

Susan Kehoe owns Browseabout Books in Rehoboth Beach, Delaware.

I t's great that you love books and want to work at a bookstore," I tell the potential employee sitting across from me. "But do you also like to clean toilets?"

It's a valid question.

People always say they'd love to open a bookstore or work in one because they have this romantic notion of walking around all day with their nose in a book or sitting in a big, overstuffed chair drinking tea and talking about Dickens.

That's not the reality. Part of the job is dealing with unexpected problems like clogged toilets and other little disasters that happen every day at the store—like sweeping sand.

A lot of sand.

Browseabout Books is located a block and a half from the

ocean, in the middle of a mile-long boardwalk. In the summer months, we have a constant influx of sand. People coming up from the beach wearing bathing suits and bikinis are covered with it—and, when making purchases, they pull moist money from strange places.

Our 13,000-square-foot store attracts a mix of locals and tourists. In addition to books and menu items from a small café, we sell a little bit of everything—toys, games, even stationery. Working with an artist, we've created a line of jig-saw puzzles and other higher-end, gift-quality items that people want to take home with them. We're big on changing up merchandise because we want everyone who comes into the store to have a unique experience.

But books are the heart of what we do, and books offer a way to escape reality and immerse the reader in another world. There are millions and millions of books out there, and people keep returning to the store because they trust our recommendations.

Especially those for kids. Everyone says kids don't read anymore, which I don't find to be true. We have so many enthusiastic kids leaving the store with stacks of books. They're staring at computer screens all day long, so having a physical book in their hands, I think, allows them an escape.

I love it when a parent comes back and says, "My kid wasn't a reader, but you guys suggested a book, and I gave it to him, and he hasn't stopped reading. It's like this whole new world has opened up for him."

Knowing we can literally change someone's life is pretty cool.

And it never gets old.

Rehoboth is known as the nation's summer capital because of its popularity with people from the DC area, which is roughly two hours away. After damages from Hurricane Sandy limited access to the beaches a little farther north in New Jersey, even more people discovered Rehoboth.

After college, I worked at a university bookstore, then became a commissioned sales rep for about forty publishers. Rehoboth was part of my sales territory. From the moment I met them, I had a great rapport with the original Browseabout owners, Steve and Barbara Crane, who opened the shop in 1975.

Over the years, Steve kept nudging, "My kids aren't interested in the business. Don't you want to take over the store from us?"

I resisted for a while, but eventually I joined them at the store, taking on more and more responsibilities until I became manager. In November 2020, my husband and I officially purchased the store from Steve and Barbara.

Seems like a great idea to buy a bookstore during a pandemic, right?

Well, we did it.

It's definitely a full-time job and then some. Thankfully,

even though my husband tries to be involved as little as possible—he has his own career—I'm so grateful that he handles all the jobs that make me weep to think about, like scheduling floor cleaners and putting in new lighting. And he does them with a smile on his face because he knows it makes me happy.

The most gratifying thing is when people come into the store and just say, "We love Browseabout so much. It's not only our favorite store in Rehoboth, it's our favorite store anywhere."

It really is great to be able to provide that for people.

Browseabout Books has seen generations of families. Kids who grew up in the store are always sending me applications for summer jobs. They could make more money waiting tables, but they want to work here because Browseabout has been a part of their lives. The resort areas are booming and there's an influx of retirees buying new homes. Some of these folks, most of them former teachers, lawyers, and other professionals, also come to the store looking for part-time work.

We're well known in beach-reading circles. Elin Hilderbrand, the bestselling author and "queen of beach reads," is a store favorite. I felt like we made it when she gave us a little name-drop in her book *Golden Girl*—her main character, an author, mentions starting her book tour at Browseabout Books.

I've known Elin for so long that when she comes in for an event, there's no awkwardness.

Which is nice. I'm *terrible* at small talk, so it's no surprise that I don't enjoy cocktail parties. But I've grown more comfortable in our bookstore environment, even when well-known

TV personalities visit the store and do author events. And politicians. We've had book signings for both President Biden and the First Lady.

Luckily, the Bidens are very approachable. They engage and interact with people. Jill Biden often comes in here alone to pick out books. She's hard to miss because of the cadre of Secret Service following her around.

Every time I see the First Lady, I think back to July 2018 and a book signing we had for Hoda Kotb, coanchor of NBC News's *Today* show and author of the inspirational book *I Really Needed This Today*. Two hundred fifty people lined up to meet her. Even Jill and Joe Biden stood in line. They wanted to stop by to say hello and deliver a bouquet of fresh-cut hydrangeas from their garden.

Like I said, I'm not good at small talk, but anytime I see the Bidens, they make me feel comfortable. I'm not nervous about making conversation.

If I can talk to them, I'm always telling myself, *I can talk to anyone*.

Sally Brewster

*Sally Brewster is the owner of Park Road Books
in Charlotte, North Carolina.*

I'm sitting in the back office, going through paperwork,
when a call comes in.

It's a reporter for *Charlotte Magazine*. They want to do a
story on us. The bookstore's doing well, and we run four successful book clubs.

"Can we send a photographer?"

"Of course," I reply. "Take as many pictures of the store as
you want."

"Actually, we want pictures of Yola. The story is about her."

"Really?" I turn to look at Yola, my twenty-five-pound
corgi–Carolina dog mix, sitting on her dog bed behind me. Her
ears perk up. She knows I'm talking about her.

I adopted Yola over a decade ago from an animal shelter

when she was a five-month-old puppy. She's our bookstore dog—I bring her to work every day. If Yola's not in the back with me, she's wandering the store, greeting customers. It's not unusual to see her sitting in our book-display front window.

Yola is *very* popular with the customers. But this is a first.

"You're writing an article about my dog?"

"Yes. Yola's been nominated for Charlottean of the year for all the work she does at your store. She brightens people's days."

She does. People come in all the time specifically to see her, sometimes even calling to ask if Yola can stay past her regularly scheduled hours—which are posted on our front door—so they can say hi.

"You don't get that type of feeling shopping online or at a big-box store," the reporter says.

As I hang up the phone and get to my feet, Yola is already off her dog bed, heading for the door.

I open the office door and she is off and running, tail wagging as she barks to let customers know she's in the store. Some look up from the shelves or their books to say hello. One woman reaches down to give Yola a quick ear scratch.

A group of smiling moms and their excited kids, all armed with books to buy, are hovering near the registers. Yola sees them, comes to a stop.

Drops to the ground and rolls onto her back.

It's the cue to let the belly-rubbing begin.

Dozens of fingers commence scratching and rubbing. Yola's in heaven.

I am too.

I call myself a Charlottean by choice, not by accident of birth. My family moved down when my dad, who worked for DuPont, was transferred in the late 1970s.

After going to grad school for history, I realize that I want to be in the book industry, and I basically bug Random House until they hire me as a Southeast sales rep. They agree, and I go to work for their Ballantine imprint. My territory is Savannah, Georgia, and North and South Carolina.

I start off with paperbacks, then move over to the independent distributor business, the people who stock airports. It isn't nearly as much fun. No one talks about the books anymore. How exciting the plots are. How beautiful the writing is. Our conversations are purely about numbers. "How many books are you going to buy?" and "How many books of such and such title sold that week?"

Bertelsmann buys out Random House. I'm offered a package to leave.

I take it. It's 1999. I'm young, and I'm looking forward to the next chapter of my life.

I get a call from the previous owner of Park Road Books, a professor, who says he's getting ready to retire.

"You should buy the bookstore from me," he says.

Are you crazy? I think. The competition is fierce. Borders, Barnes & Noble, Joseph-Beth, Books-A-Million, and Media Play, as well as several established independent bookstores, dominate the retail landscape.

The owner, I can tell, really needs help. I offer to run the bookstore for him until he finds an owner.

Two weeks into the job, my attitude changes. I do want to own this store—and I've got to find a way to make it happen.

I just have to believe.

Charlotte has a good balance of conservatives and liberals. It's a very vibrant city in a great location, between the beaches and the mountains. I buy the bookstore in 2003 and hope to make it a place for everybody. My plan works, but it's tough going.

When people tell me they want to open a bookstore because they like to read and love books, I always question, "Well, can you run a business?"

Luckily, I really enjoy the business aspect. Because there are some brutal years.

When the recession hits in 2008, a lot of the big-name retail bookstores declare bankruptcy. Our sales drop for the next two years, to the point where I'm wondering if Park Road Books, which first opened in 1977, is going to be able to stay in business.

I insist on paying for my employees' health insurance. Stopping that benefit would free up some cash, but I refuse to go down that road. My husband and I live frugally to keep this important benefit for employees. I pay way above minimum wage and still buy my employees gas cards, pizza, sandwiches, and other supplemental perks.

Then something amazing happens.

The people of Charlotte band together and decide to save

their local stores. Park Road Books turns into a small community, a place where people can come and browse, discuss books with others, and get book recommendations.

And visit Yola, obviously.

When the pandemic hits in 2020, I turn to my brother, who is also my manager, and say, "I know how to survive a recession, but I'm not sure how we're going to survive a pandemic."

The state announces a thirty-day shutdown. The governor says that bookstores are essential, but the city of Charlotte says they're not. Park Road Books will, unfortunately, be closed, but my brother and I quickly realize that there will be no sitting around on the couch. The next day, we're busier than ever with online and phone orders.

The phone never stops ringing. We ship orders and arrange pickups. Our store is long and skinny, and, like every good bookstore, the back rooms are a mess. We're in an old, strip-mall-style shopping center. People pull up to the front curb and we run books out to them.

It's the hardest I've ever worked in my life.

Two weeks into the shutdown, I get a phone call from the police.

"You've been reported for letting people in the store," says the policeman on the other end of the line. "Customers aren't allowed inside your business."

"We're not. We're absolutely not," I say, and explain what we're doing.

The policeman is very nice. Sympathetic. But according to

the rules, we're not allowed to run books out to customers. I stick to mail delivery only.

I still can't believe someone narked on us.

But at least we know how to survive a pandemic. Now I just worry that something else is going to happen.

In December, it's time for our annual book tree.

The tree is filled with slips of paper—book requests from children in need. Customers are given a big discount if they buy a book—or books—for these children, whose teachers help them write thank-you notes.

When I read something like *Thank you. This is the first book I've ever owned,* it makes me want to weep. It breaks my heart that some kids don't own books, and some kids don't have a home to own books in. We try to do everything we possibly can to help the community because we're all in this together. We're not individuals. We're Charlotteans, North Carolinians, Americans.

We're getting to be more of a literary town, with a lot of new bookstores that have just opened. I'm thrilled with that. We're all family. We will do anything we can to help each other out.

"Excuse me."

I turn and see a little girl who is about seven years old.

"I saw that dogs are allowed in the store."

"Yes," I say. "Do you have a dog?"

She shakes her head. "Are other animals allowed?"

"We've had someone bring a cat on a leash. One time we had an owl in here for a presentation." And there was the time a children's author brought chickens to her book reading.

"I have a tortoise," the girl says. "His name is Shelly. Can I bring him in?"

"Absolutely."

I watch her walk away, thinking, *She's seven. She's going to bring in a stuffed animal*.

The girl returns with an actual tortoise.

Shelly becomes a regular customer.

P. J. Gardiner

P. J. Gardiner is the collection development librarian at the Wake County Public Library System in Raleigh, North Carolina.

My most cherished childhood memory is of being read to. Whether it was Mom or my teacher reading the stories, I just loved listening to the words and seeing pictures in the books.

In my small hometown in Indiana, there's a historic Carnegie library. I get my first job there as a page. I really like flipping through the books as I shelve them. They have different smells. I open one book and think, *It smells like pickles.*

Watching my supervisor do story time also gets me thinking, *Well, maybe I want to do that someday.*

After earning my undergraduate degree in school media services and my master's degree in library science, I have a brief stint at a school library before moving over to the public libraries, where I serve as a children's librarian doing story times, just like the supervisor I admired so much.

At my very first story time in the public library, I sit down with this group of fifteen or so kids, three or four years old, and their parents. I'm nervous and I think, *Okay, I'm going to start off strong.*

I welcome everyone and ask, "Is this anybody's first time?"

One dad looks at me and says, "Yours."

Yep. You are so right, Dad.

Most of us librarians know going in that one of our roles is to be a champion of the freedom to read. Most of us are also mild-mannered people. We're not combative or necessarily ready to take on controversial situations. So, while we talk about all the theories around censorship in library school, to be faced with a confrontation about which books belong on library shelves is shocking.

My first major encounter happens when I am young, maybe twenty-four, twenty-five, right after the Columbine school shooting.

I'm working at a middle school in North Carolina when the school principal comes to me and says, "It's come to my attention that we have this book, and I want you to take it off the shelf. It doesn't have any place in our library."

The book is *Killing Mr. Griffin,* a young adult novel by Lois Duncan about some teens who, as a prank, kidnap a teacher, who then has a medical emergency and dies. The book is really about their remorse and a reflection on what they did and how wrong it was and how even though his death was not their intent, it happened anyway.

I ask the principal, "Did you read the whole book? It's not about killing a teacher."

She shuts me down. "No, I don't need to read the whole book. It just doesn't have a place in our library."

I really don't know what to do. Some supportive colleagues at the school say to me, "Okay, there is a committee process in place. Everyone on the committee has to read the book, discuss the book as a whole, and make a decision."

It is not the principal's decision, but she pretty much makes it impossible to follow the process. I'm young, I'm unwilling to go up against an authority figure, so I decide it's time for me to find another job.

People feel very strongly about protecting children from dangerous ideas. The pressure has always been there. There's always some level of somebody in a role who wants a book removed for whatever reason.

It's not the majority of people, but it's a small, noisy, well-organized group of people who have really exploded the issue in our public library system. Ours has twenty-three branches and the total number of print volumes we'll buy in a fiscal year is about 340,000. We used to get very few challenges from the public. This year, we've already had a lot, and they're mostly focused on children's books.

What hasn't changed is that people love libraries. They're community places, places where people can gather. That's how I always see the library. When I walk into one of our library locations now, I see tutoring happening, I see people sitting one-on-one with a librarian, getting assistance and filling out a job application. It's very vibrant and lively.

I don't see the library going away at all. We'll just have to keep up with whatever comes next and evolve with what our citizens want.

We hope they continue to want what we provide: lifelong learning and joy.

Nancy Moore

Nancy Moore is the store manager at Barnes &
Noble in North Dartmouth, Massachusetts.

A room without books is like a body without a soul." That's
the line printed on our new in-store table signs.

When I go to somebody's house and they have a bookcase,
I like to peruse it and see what titles they've chosen. Will they
have the latest nonfiction, or World War II historical novels, or
poetry? Once, I spot Yoko Ono's book of conceptual art, *Grape-*
fruit, on my friend's brother's shelf, and I remember my own
copy from back in, like, 1970. *Okay,* I think, *kindred spirits*.

If they don't have any books sitting around, I think, *Oh*.

I've been with Barnes & Noble for forty years, in six stores.
Sometimes I'm surprised that I haven't moved on to different
things, but the books are always changing, the staff is always

changing, the community is always changing, so the job has always been interesting and rewarding.

Everybody I know reads, and we talk books all the time. I have to remind myself that I'm living in a bubble. I'm always astounded to hear about the number of people who don't read. I've taken to double-checking those sobering statistics compiled by Literacy Inc., that 33 percent of high school graduates never pick up another book, and that 42 percent of college grads don't either. Oh yeah, and apparently 80 percent of American families did not purchase a book this year. I can't imagine what people do without books in their lives.

When somebody is struggling with a personal issue, our job as booksellers becomes really important. That's when I feel we are able to help the most.

An older gentleman comes into the store. He's just lost his wife and he's grieving. Still, he's worried about how to handle the condolences. My business development person and I sit with him. *Well, you probably don't need to send a reply to these people, but to these others you do.* And we help him find a book that shows how to compose the appropriate thank-you letters.

On the other end, when news of a customer's divorce made it into the local paper and then a week or two later she comes in buying *The Joy of Cheesecake* and *The Joy of Sex,* I think, *Good for you, getting back out there again!*

We let dogs come into the store as long as their people keep them on leash. My staff loves dogs, so of course, all work stops.

Maddie, an older yellow Lab, is a store favorite. She's been battling cancer and going through chemo. Her owners, a mother and daughter, say, "Maddie, you want to go to the bookstore?" And boy does she perk up and come right to the door.

We get a call: "Maddie wants to come in to say goodbye."

They bring the dog in one last time.

One of my booksellers calls me, crying, and says, "Maddie's family asked me to come over. Can I come to work late?"

"Of course," I say, thinking of the dog who loved to come to the bookstore.

Another customer, Polly McNamara, is one of these wiry old women who walks everywhere wearing a little cap. The whole store gets to know her. She brings in bagels and coffee when she comes to browse the romance section for her favorite authors. Every Christmas she sends me a Trader Joe's or Whole Foods gift card.

"Polly's on the phone!" one of the staff says when Polly calls looking for gifts for her nieces and nephews.

Then the calls from Polly stop, so I call her.

No answer.

I call again. The phone is disconnected.

We are all pretty upset, but I think, *Well, her nieces and nephews don't know that they should tell me if something's happened.*

About a month later, a call comes over my headset. "Polly's on the phone!" And we are all just ready to cheer. She'd fallen ill and was calling from rehab but was still going. She's really quite the spirit.

My staff, they all read different genres. So I've picked up

some books that I wouldn't normally have read, which is always interesting. Even when I'm in family gatherings or social settings, I always end up discussing books, asking people what they're reading, recommending new titles to them. I tell people about how I choose a good audiobook for my commute. A favorite is Daniel Silva and his hero, Gabriel Allon. I get in the car and say, "Oh, yay. I have someone to keep me company!"

Once in a while, I hear people say about a particular book, *Oh, I'm struggling.* And I remind them, *There are so many good books out there that if this one's not working for you, if you're not enjoying it, don't finish it.* You know? One of the best problems about working in a bookstore is that we all see so much and buy so many, and we all have so many books in our to-be-read pile.

My home gets so full of print books that I have to pass them along. I'll give a book to someone in my yoga class, and they'll ask, "Do you want it back?"

"No, no, no," I say. "Keep it going."

Erin Blake

Erin Blake works as a planner-distributor for
Books-A-Million, based in Birmingham,
Alabama.

People come into bookstores to touch the books and to feel the books, and to see what's new. They come in to soak up the books.

As much as people complain about social media, it's definitely helped the book industry. Engagement online draws people into bookstores to get these books.

People post, "Oh, I just read this great book," or they talk about their favorite authors, or they show links to author events. It gets authors' names out there.

The biggest and most helpful trend is BookTok. That is huge. I've never seen anything like it. We have books that are ten, fifteen years old that we can't keep in stock because they're trending on BookTok. What's interesting is, when it comes to kids' books, the books they end up taking home, the books they are coming back to, are the ones parents remember from when they were kids, like Dr. Seuss and Junie B. Jones and Magic Tree House.

Movies based on books also help with book sales—the movies are never *as* good, so people want to go back and read the original books. The books might have come out five or ten years ago, but because everything seems fresh, they're really popping off.

My kids' and teen buyer does the new title buys, and then she sends me a list of which books she's bought and how many copies of each. What I do is, I look at all the stores, chain-wide, and, based on their sales, I decide how much goes into what store and who gets it and who doesn't. So I have the fun job.

I just love planning. I am the planner for kids', teen, and mass-market fiction. I have the best groups. Making projections, trying to figure out what's going to sell, what's not going to sell, getting the right stuff in the right store. It's fun. It's exciting to me.

When I first started working in the bookstore, the kids' department was only a couple of sections, maybe four or five small sections. Now we have giant sections. Fiction, of course, is the number one category, but the young adult section is huge and it's great. Nowadays, most of our stores have ten to fourteen sections of young adult, which is fabulous. A lot of adults read young adult books because they touch on so many different genres. Half of our people who work here love the young adult books.

I was a teenager myself when I started in the industry, about forty years ago.

My father was a big reader, and on Sundays he and I would go to Bookland, in a little strip center in Daytona Beach, Florida, right next door to my high school. My father would always get me a book.

One day, I was talking to the bookstore manager, and I asked, "Do you hire fifteen-year-olds?"

She answered, "As a matter of fact, we do. Are you interested?"

"Oh gosh, yeah," I said.

She smiled. "I know you're always in here."

I filled out an application and started that same night. That began my career with Bookland, which eventually became Books-A-Million. I was nineteen when I became the store manager. I went to one year of college but then stopped because I was working and didn't have time. I moved up, moved up, moved up, moved up.

I just love my career. I couldn't work at a job I didn't like. The work is the same every day, but the excitement over upcoming books makes it seem new. When the publishers come in for seasonal presentation, we're like little kids at Christmas. "Oh, I can't wait for that one!" And we make notes, *I've got to get this book. I've got to get this book. I've got to get this book.*

I'm excited about James Patterson's new Alex Cross book. I

love those books, but the biggest James Patterson fan was my mother. Oh my God. She was rabid. It was hysterical.

So I would get the book and read it, and then give it to her. She was like a pit bull. "Are you done yet? Are you done yet? Can I have it now? Can I have it now?"

"Here you go," I'd say, but that was just the beginning.

She would read the book and she had a little posse, a funny little group of retired nuns who were rabid James Patterson fans too.

They were very cute about it, but just like my mom bugged me, they too would constantly call her, asking, "Are you done yet? Are you done yet?"

My mom would tell them, "I will give you the book when I'm done."

Most books she'd drive over to them as soon as she turned the last page. But if the book was too risqué, she wouldn't give it to them. "This is too much for you," she would tell them. "You can't read this one."

That was the best book group. My mom passed away last year, sadly. I still think to myself, *Aw, she would be so excited to read the brand-new one.*

I feel like more kids are experiencing a love of books now, especially little kids. Whenever I visit family, I don't take stuffed animals or toys or video games. I bring bags of books. They'd rather have a book, and it just makes my heart happy that they love books as much as I do.

Right before Christmas this year, I take my nephew and a friend of his to the movies. Afterward, I give them a choice between going to a restaurant with video games or to the bookstore. Both of them say, "Let's go to Books-A-Million."

So we go walking in, and there's a cart in the front of the store filled with Diary of a Wimpy Kid and Dog Man and Cat Kid books. Both kids go running.

My nephew's little friend says, "Oh my God! I've got to have this book. I have to have this book. I have to have this book."

My nephew echoes, "I need to have it too!"

I have tears in my eyes. I am so excited.

They spend half an hour going through books, narrowing it down to their top choice.

I say to my sister-in-law, "You don't know how happy this makes me."

McKenna Jordan

McKenna Jordan is the owner of Murder By The Book in Houston, Texas, and a consultant for Minotaur Books at Macmillan Publishers.

Bookselling is this weird world where it's kind of like rainbows and unicorns and magic, but it's also a business.

My job is to discover new authors. To find amazing new voices and to put those books into as many hands as I can.

Customers know about the number one *New York Times* bestsellers. What they don't know about is the brand-new historical mystery set in India that they're going to absolutely love because of the charming characters. So those are the books that I seek out as the proprietor of Murder By The Book, one of the oldest and largest mystery specialty bookstores in the country.

I read Paula Hawkins's *The Girl on the Train* six months

before it comes out and just keep nagging the publicist, "This book is amazing. We want to order hundreds of copies. You have to bring her over for a tour." We hand-sell 600 or 800 copies of *The Girl on the Train* before it becomes *The Girl on the Train*. It's so fun to be able to do that and make a difference very, very early on in an author's career.

I love doing this. I love reading a great book and recommending something that people haven't heard of before, getting to have interesting conversations with customers. And once they've read and loved it, they come back. They're so happy that you found something new for them.

I first came to the store as a customer, a college kid finishing up an English literature degree and shopping on weekends for cheap finds in the used-book section.

Every time I come in, I ask if there are any openings on staff.

The answer is always the same. *No, because no one ever leaves.*

Finally, they change up the Saturday schedule. Four hours a week become available. I'm hired. My first day of work is January 11, 2003. That same day, an abandoned Rottweiler puppy finds its way to the store. Soon the whole staff is out back watching a manager named David coax the frightened dog to eat a few bites of his sandwich.

I'm at the register all alone, answering customers' questions by myself on my first day. I learn right away that working at this store is going to take some hustle.

By the summer, I'm covering people's vacations and basically working full-time. David and I become fast friends. He takes the puppy home and names him Travis. We go out after work for drinks—cosmos for me, margaritas on the rocks with salt for David—and talk about our days at the store. And books. Always books.

Though it takes a few years for us to notice and then do something about it, David and I fall in love. We marry in 2008 at Dryburgh Abbey in Scotland. The *Houston Chronicle* does a great piece on us, "A Storybook Marriage."

The original owner of Murder By The Book, who started the store in 1980, is making her retirement plans. She's always wanted to leave the store to David but sees that he doesn't have any kind of business sense. And that I do.

In January 2009, I purchase the store from her. I'm twenty-six. David and I are married, and happy here together at Murder By The Book. He has his own publishing company, Busted Flush, and I have the store. That kind of team effort seems like a good plan.

Then David dies unexpectedly on September 13, 2010. He's thirty-eight.

Life takes us in some weird directions, right?

David was a force of nature, and very well loved by all the authors and customers. Six hundred people attend his memorial service. People fly in from all over the country, all over the world. Lee Child flies in from the UK.

People in the crime fiction community are very supportive. "Read a book in his honor," the publisher of *Mystery Scene* magazine suggests. In 2011, Bouchercon, the annual World

Mystery Convention, establishes the David Thompson Memorial Special Service Award for basically being a good guy or woman in the field of mystery.

I have to very quickly figure out, *Okay, here we are. I've got staff that depend on me. Everything has to go on. It's my store and I need to make it work. Let me figure it out.*

My staff is wonderful, but it's not easy. It takes a really long time before the store finds its way. Still, I remain its sole owner. I'm just now over forty. So the store's been a big part of my life for more than twenty years. We're in a new era.

We're constantly trying to hand-sell books to people who want more great books.

We keep databases of everything that our customers buy. We hustle. We're a *New York Times* reporting bookstore. That matters to publishers. In short, we sell a lot of books. But we also develop relationships with people. We know the names of our customers, their children, and what's happening in their lives. And in among those conversations, we recommend books that we know they're going to love. It is definitely a community.

We have a well-run, well-oiled machine for author events, from the presale signing to how we do the line afterward. And we try very hard to make sure we sell a lot of books, make sure that the experience is good all around, both for our customers and for the authors.

The crowd is happy and the author signs a lot of books and sells a lot of books, consistently some of the highest figures on tour.

Authors want to come back, and they'll tell their publicists.

We push for a long time to get one particular author to the store. "Can we get James Patterson? Can we get James Patterson?"

And finally we get to host James Patterson. As you would imagine, we have a huge turnout, with people lined up for a good while. It was all very smooth and organized. He was a delight. Everyone was happy. So that was an amazing night.

Book signings so often are. When people come in to meet their favorite author, we stress to them, "If you want to keep seeing authors come through here, support us so that we can stay around and keep doing this. Come to the store, have a good time—and buy the book."

The best is when customers leave with a stack of books, saying, "This is the most wonderful talk I've ever heard and thank you so much for hosting it."

Beth Jarrell

Beth Jarrell is reference librarian and digital archivist at Sanibel Public Library in Sanibel, Florida.

Libraries are about books, but not only about books. People think of libraries as giant repositories for books and of librarians as people who sit around and read all day, two concepts that could not be further from the truth.

I grew up in Saskatchewan, Canada, where visits to our local public library were the highlight of my life. I always found something to read at the library. I was the kid hiding under the covers with the flashlight reading late into the night. "Just one more chapter, please, just one more chapter."

I get my undergrad degree in journalism from the University of Toronto, then land a job in a town called Swift Current, Saskatchewan, where, for six hours a day, I DJ at a classic-rock radio station and also do online news and multimedia storytelling. Journalism is really cool, but I decide I want to be under a different part of the information umbrella. I enroll in the library science master's program at the University of Washington in Seattle. I quickly learn that the curriculum is geared to highly theoretical skill sets.

My first week, I'm freaking out. I don't know if this is where I should be. I don't know if this is going to be the right fit.

One of my professors says, "Most of you are here because you are the person that people turn to when they need to find something. Whether it's your parents or a sibling or a friend or a coworker, you're the person that people turn to and say, 'Hey, can you find me information on whatever.'"

I calm down and realize, *Oh yeah, that's me, that's absolutely me.*

No matter where I end up after graduation, I'm confident that I'll always be that person who can find the information.

I want to stay in the United States for as long as I can. I love this country. I'm very proud to live here. Fortunately, if you do your master's degree in the United States, you can stay to work in your field.

I start looking for jobs, thinking, *Hey, maybe I can land in Sanibel Island, Florida. I'm familiar with the place.*

My grandfather often wintered in Sanibel. If you're from our part of Canada, it's basically a rule that you have to go to

Florida for the winter at least once. I've been coming to Sanibel every year since the mid-1990s. Despite being 3,000 miles apart, my grandfather and I bonded over classic Western novels like Larry McMurtry's *Lonesome Dove*. I was a big horse girl, so I read *Lonesome Dove* in eighth grade. That book not only opened up a world of adult literature to me, it gave me and my grandfather something to talk about over the phone.

I walk into the library in Sanibel, Florida, with my résumé in hand and beg for an internship. What was supposed to be a six-month internship turns into a full-time job. Four years later, here I am.

From my first day on the job, what stands out to me is the librarians' freedom to start new initiatives. Sanibel Public continues to be one of *Library Journal*'s America's Star Libraries for public library service, meaning it's always very highly rated, has great support from the community, and is really innovative in the ways it always pushes boundaries and always evolves in what it means to be a library.

Yes, Google's great and ChatGPT is an interesting wave of the future, but neither has the human element of being able to sort and find. We offer bird-watching kits and we recently added a tool library so people can check out tools, hammers, screwdrivers, and we also have Tech IT Out, a rental service for laptops, GoPros, and Wi-Fi hot spots.

My favorite thing is helping people. Handing someone a book with the power to change their lives is magical because, oftentimes, it does.

So does restoring a lost part of their past, whether it's

finding an obituary of someone's father they thought they'd never find again or having a woman come in and say, "Hey, I've heard my great-grandmother used to live on this island. I've never seen a picture of her. Do you know anything about her?"

I hand her a photo of her great-grandmother.

Hurricane Ian strikes in the last week of September 2022. It's an intense Category 4 storm. Sanibel Island is under mandatory evacuation. Two of our staff stay on to ride out the storm. I'm not that brave. I drive home to Canada for a month.

Libraries are information centers, but in the immediate aftermath of Ian, all we have are pictures that show the front doors blasted off the library and about three feet of water inside. Our front lobby is completely gutted. Our main entrance is gutted. Our secondary entrance is gutted.

We are thinking, *Oh God, what are we going to walk into?* As an archivist, I'm asking myself, *How are these climate-controlled archival materials going to hold up?*

There's one bridge onto the island and one bridge off and that's it. The causeway is washed away. Some people take boats over. There is no other way to reach the island until the Army Corps of Engineers comes in and makes emergency repairs.

Everyone is desperate for information, any piece of news we can get about our homes and the place we live.

I come back to the island in early November, along with a couple of coworkers. "We're just going to do it," we say. "We're going to figure this out and serve people the best that we can."

The library is right next door to city hall and the police station, so we're on the newly restored main power grid. Day in, day out, we are on the ground, and we never stop our service. We get out on social media, promoting our ebooks and audiobooks, helping people find information, and even serving as a hurricane information center, sharing any details we have.

People come in our doors and start crying. "Thank God," they say. "The library feels normal."

A lot of our neighbors have lost everything they own. These are people who've worked hard their entire lives and saved up enough money to buy a house on Sanibel, live their dream. Now their condos or bungalows have ten feet of water inside and they're camping in their front yards.

They're already up to an eleven dealing with insurance people and plumbers and construction. They need access to printers and the internet, but they also need someone to talk to for a bit. While they print insurance documents and have our notary sign them, people tell us how they've lost their entire family histories, their father's boyhood pictures and documents. As an archivist, I'm reminded of the days when town records were kept in churches. If a church burned down, there went the records.

Fortunately, our library building is two stories. Our first

floor, with our meeting room and our lobby and our cataloging department, will need to be rebuilt. But the entire main collection, all the books, are up on the second floor. It looks unchanged upstairs. We have mold testing done, we have everything checked over, and our collection is perfectly safe.

We haven't lost a single book.

Jessica Claudio

Jessica Claudio is the head store manager at the Barnes & Noble in Staten Island, New York.

I don't judge anyone's taste in books. I just love book passion. It doesn't matter *what* you like to read, as long as you love to read.

In Staten Island, we are part of New York City, but we are literally an island unto ourselves. My Barnes & Noble is the only bookstore on the island. Anyone who wants a book these days on Staten Island has to come to my store.

I got into the book business when I was sixteen. My sister was the café lead at our local Barnes & Noble, which had opened two years prior. And I applied for and got hired into a seasonal position, which has now lasted a little over eighteen years, with over ten years as a manager.

Each individual Barnes & Noble store manager is also a business owner. We get to make our stores fit where we live.

Like I say, we're the only place around to buy books, so we're big on a variety of subjects, from contemporary fiction and romance to history, from mystery and thriller to spirituality. Our loyal customer base represents all sorts of different minds coming together.

Being a big, commercial bookstore, we try to keep it as commercial as possible. Though when all the Barnes & Noble stores got new lines of leather-bound, collectible, giftable classics, it raised interesting questions.

What is considered a classic? What belongs in the classics section? A case could be made for putting most of the store in "Classics," so where do we draw the line?

People look under classics when they're purchasing summer reading titles for their kids' school assignments, which raises even more questions, like, "How could we leave out *The Great Gatsby*?" Since in our store, the classics section is adjacent to fiction, we keep it as fiction classics, but even then, "How modern do you go?" It's an ongoing debate.

I love being on the selling floor talking about books with people, talking to my booksellers. Though when I come in for my shift, I go straight into the back room.

"What exciting books came in today?" I ask whoever's working, because there are always exciting books coming in.

"Oh, yay," I'll say, if it's a book that customers have been asking about, or a book that has been out of stock. Or maybe it's a book that another Barnes & Noble posted on social media, a book that I ordered because I thought it looked cool.

I've never been a back-office manager. Whenever I have tasks that require me to be in the back office, I become the biggest procrastinator. Because I just love being on the selling floor, talking about books with my customers and my booksellers.

When hiring a bookseller, my first question is "Do you like to read?"

Then "What do you like to read?"

If I'm not familiar with their favorites, I might say, "I haven't checked that one out yet. Why should I read it?" And we go from there.

I'm not sure how much of a connection can be forged between a grocery clerk loving the same oranges as a hungry shopper, or an apparel salesperson and a fashion-conscious customer both loving the newest pair of pants. But at the bookstore, part of the job is talking about interests, in order to figure out what people are looking for. We want to help you find the book that will connect with you. Sometimes we've got to ask a lot of questions to get there.

One of my customers comes in and asks me to look up a title.

"Oh, we just got two copies of this book in the store," I say. "Let me see if I can find it." And I do.

In passing, he mentions that his name is Michael DeConzo. He is the author.

He is almost shy about it, but I get so excited. I am very passionate about helping out Staten Island authors, hosting book signings and things like that. Those are the people who support our store, and I want in turn to represent their books to the community.

"Oh, let's get you to sign your book," I say. "And we can take a picture and post it on our Instagram. And you can post it on yours and let your friends and family know that we carry your book here in Barnes & Noble."

His friends and his family really show their support. They keep buying it off the shelf. So we are constantly ordering a few copies. He and his wife frequently have lunch in our café, where I stop in for my favorite latte. Whenever I see him and I know we have fresh, unsigned stock, I'll say, "Hey, do you want to come sign some of these?"

One of our other customers, Mike, has a special routine. He always carefully puts away whatever books he's been looking at.

"I can do that for you," I tell him. "This is what I get paid to do."

"Oh no," he says. "I worked at a bookshop in college. I can do it. I can do it."

One day, Mike rushes in, frantic, looking for a little plush toy he bought here at the store for his son. "Puppy Duppy" is missing, so I help him find a new Puppy Duppy to replace the one his son lost. And that son is now college age. Because I've known them for years and years and years, seeing Mike and his family at the store gets me feeling almost sentimental.

Another time, a teenage girl comes in visibly upset. "I need something good to read," she says. "I need to get my mind off of things."

"Maybe you can talk to me," I say. "What's going on?"

She starts to tell me about how her cat had a litter of kittens, and one of them didn't make it. And she is just sobbing. We talk quietly for a little while and I recommend some books to clear her thoughts of losing that kitten.

I like to think she feels just a little better walking out that day.

People tell me all sorts of things because they're so comfortable in the bookstore. A woman asks for books on pregnancy. She also shares a secret. Her daughter-in-law is pregnant, she says, but doesn't want to tell anyone yet. But, she says, "I can tell you, because I don't know you, that I'm going to be a grandma for the first time!" I squeal, and we are both just so excited.

Bookstores represent learning and ideas, curiosity. I get emotional thinking about my son potentially growing up in a place without a bookstore, without a place he'll be able to browse for whatever he might be interested in or whatever finds him.

This store needs to stick around and do well.

It's important to me. It's important to all of us.

PART TWO

I could talk about books forever.

Carolyn Foote

Carolyn Foote lives in Austin, Texas, and works as a consultant for libraries across the country. In 2013, she was selected for the White House Champion of Change award. She was also the recipient of the American Association of School Librarians Collaborative School Library Award in 2019 and the AASL Intellectual Freedom Award in 2022.

Having a good library is not political.

A good library will have books on vegetarianism *and* on hunting. A good library will have books on *every* religion. A good library will have books about *all* eras of history, from ancient Rome to the Civil War to the Holocaust. A good library will have books about different countries, different cultures, and different life experiences.

I became a school librarian in 1991, after ten years as a high school English teacher. Becoming a librarian was the perfect melding of my interests. I've always felt at home with high school students. I just love being around them. I love teaching them, discussing books, helping foster a love of reading. I also love research and technology, from doing professional development for our teachers to being an early advocate for technology use in libraries.

I made the right decision. I was in the right place.

For the next twenty-nine years, I work in the same small suburban school district in Texas, the last fourteen of which I spend as the district librarian.

In 2021 I notice an unprecedented—and frightening—trend of activists and conservative groups demanding that certain books be removed from libraries and classrooms. Their primary targets are books dealing with diversity and equality.

By the fall of that year, I'm also seeing books that deal with racism or include topics like sex and sexual identity, puberty, reproduction, pregnancy, and abortion being challenged.

It's alarming.

Every school district has a selection policy and a reconsideration policy that comes into play if a book is challenged. Trained librarians are well versed in these policies. Over the previous nearly three decades, my school district received three book challenges—not even for library books but in English classrooms. In comparison, high school libraries across the country are now receiving anywhere from ten to more than fifty challenges per *year*.

To make matters worse, school districts are bending to political pressure to censor books involving race and LGBTQ issues. Some school districts are now altering their library policies—or completely ignoring them.

I'm concerned about the vulnerability of our students of color, our LGBTQ students, and our students with LGBTQ parents. They're thrust into the middle of a political battle when all they're doing is trying to exist. I feel very concerned about what message we're sending by banning books that reflect their lived experience.

When a book is challenged, the first step is an informal discussion with the parent who lodged the complaint. My job—every librarian's job—is to listen to the parent or parents, try to alleviate their concerns, and help them figure out the best way to handle the matter with their child.

Librarians believe parents have a say when it comes to what their child reads. But if a parent comes in and says, "We don't want any children to read such-and-such book," that's setting the standard for someone else's family.

Different families view things differently.

And that's the catch in all of this.

Usually, complaints are dropped. But if a parent proceeds to file a formal complaint with the district, a committee of librarians, teachers, administrators, and other parents is assembled to read the book or books and make a judgment.

These policies have stood the test of time for the last fifty years.

But the activist groups are growing larger, stronger, bolder, and louder by the day.

I listen to a school board meeting in Texas where a conservative group proposes banning any book in a middle school library that includes illustrations of the human body.

My brow furrows. If that happens, reproductions of artwork by Michelangelo, for example, would be banned. How could you have an art book in the library?

The answer is, you couldn't.

This group at the school board meeting suggests using a rating system like the one that exists for movies. It would be a massive task to create a state-level review board to read and rate every single book—plus, who, exactly, would oversee it?

It would need to be overseen by a fair, judicious body.

In late October 2021, just as students who've had their education disrupted by the COVID-19 pandemic are beginning to return to classrooms, Texas Representative Matt Krause compiles a sixteen-page list of 850 fiction and nonfiction books that he believes "make students feel discomfort."

Some believe Krause's actions to be both a publicity stunt and an attention-grabbing political tactic during a crowded primary race.

The president of the Texas State Teachers Association releases a statement calling Krause's list a "disturbing and political overreach" and "an obvious attack on diversity and an attempt to score political points at the expense of our children's education."

I need to do something.

It's important for librarians to know they're not alone. Book challenges make us feel singled out and isolated, as though we've done something wrong. My colleagues and I want to create an online support space, a network with online resources and knowledgeable, understanding people who can offer guidance.

Creating such a space will take time. My colleagues and I want to push back against what's happening *now*.

Becky Calzada, a library services coordinator, and I work with two other colleagues to brainstorm ideas. We decide to launch a guerrilla social media campaign to help support not only librarians and educators, but also students and authors. Everyone deserves a voice.

We decide on the hashtag #FReadom—combining *freedom* and *read*—and create a little logo.

"What do you think about doing a hashtag takeover of the Texas Legislature?" Becky suggests. Insiders have told me that several of these Texas legislators don't actually feel strongly about the issue; they just see it as a convenient tool to rile up parents and get votes.

"That's brilliant, that's perfect," I text back.

Our plan is to coordinate having people share positive messages about meaningful books on diversity that have impacted their lives, using book covers and the hashtags #FReadom and #txlege, for the Texas Legislature.

To my amazement, over 13,000 tweets go out that day and #FReadom trends at number six on Twitter—clear examples of the desire people have to support inclusive libraries and inclusive reading titles.

The Texas Library Association issues a statement condemning censorship and offers to its members webinars, training sessions, and a designated hotline for librarians.

#FReadom has started a movement.

#FReadom becomes #FReadomFighters. We create a Twitter page and a website. Constantly updating resources for librarians, parents, students, and communities who want to speak up against censorship is a lot of work. It's also a labor of love.

Censorship is growing by the day, becoming even louder and more flagrant not only in Texas but in states across the country. In March 2022, Florida governor Ron DeSantis signs House Bill 1467, legislation that allows parents to "make decisions about what materials their children are exposed to in school," and in April 2022, Georgia governor Brian Kemp signs Senate Bill 226 into law, giving school principals only ten business days to make decisions on challenged books.

Where do we draw the line in terms of intellectual freedom and First Amendment rights?

The library is voluntary—no one is forcing children to

read, but refusing students access feels un-American to me. Students and their families deserve to have choice: for students to pick up a particular title and for their families to say they ought to put it back. Libraries don't make parenting decisions, and parents shouldn't make library choices for everyone else's children.

It's a slippery slope when concerns about challenged books go from worries over explicit content to fears that children will learn uncomfortable facts about history. Why challenge books about the Holocaust or Japanese internment camps? What's behind challenges to books about race and racism?

The hope I see now is in community groups starting to push back, showing up at school board meetings, getting organized in groups and circulating important information. Censorship fights are dependent on communities coming out to support intellectual freedom and on students participating in advocacy.

It feels like people are starting to wake up to this more and more, understanding that we need to stand up for our libraries and our librarians.

They need our support more than ever.

Cody Higgins

*Cody Higgins is the store manager at Barnes &
Noble in Dothan, Alabama.*

My mom likes to tell the story of when I was getting ready for kindergarten and throwing a huge fit because I didn't know how to read yet. I was sure everyone else was going to know how to read already, but I didn't know how. Once I did go to kindergarten, and they taught me, I kept on reading from there.

In my spare time, I'm usually reading. I always have a book with me. I read to escape. I want to experience worlds I'll never really live in, like with dragons or Greek gods. I get very involved in the stories that I read. I laugh, I cry. I'm sure my dogs think I'm crazy because I'll be sitting at home reading, then all of a sudden I'll just burst out laughing.

It's the warmest feeling to make a recommendation that connects with a reader. A ten-year-old boy and his mom come into the store. The boy loves Harry Potter and Percy Jackson books, so he's looking for more in that vein. Those are some of my favorites too, so I recommend a new book for him—and he decides to sit down right there on the floor and start reading. The kid gets like four chapters into the book before they even leave. Just seeing him walk out, hugging that book, it sends warmth right through me. It's so validating—we get invested in these books, and it means so much to tell people, "Yeah, I like that one," and see that they like it too.

Outside of the store, I mainly spend time at home with my dogs. Not long after one of them passes away after thirteen years, a customer comes in telling me that she's looking for picture books to help explain pet loss to her kids. I know just how to help her.

When I first started with Barnes & Noble ten years ago, I was a humongous introvert. I did not want to interact with anyone, did not want anything to do with the public. But I love talking about books. And I have the most amazing mentors and managers who support and empower me, and they helped me realize that whether it's a customer or a fellow bookseller, we're all just excited to be talking about books. So I started to become more outgoing.

As a manager, I try to help others in the same way. One of my recent bookseller hires barely talked at all during the interview, but I decide to take a chance and hire him. Now, after working with him, he's to the point where he's having full conversations with customers. I've seen him open up so much.

Bookstores are so much more than just retail.

They're about connecting with people.

I easily spend forty hours a week with the booksellers in my store. I've worked at a gas station, I've worked at a DirecTV call center, and I've never experienced this sense of comradery anywhere else. In the break room, people let their guard down, get emotional, whether it's someone having a horrible breakup or experiencing a problem with their family. We say, "All right, let's get you some chocolate and some coffee from the café." Then we'll go in the back, and we'll sit for a few minutes and talk about it. We're there for each other.

Even when I go to Dallas to visit a couple of friends who also work for Barnes & Noble, I ask them, "What bookstores do you have here? What can I go visit?"

They give me a list of chains and independents, and I spend my whole time visiting bookstores and eating. I get to relax with friends, *and* I get to be around more books. It's the best vacation.

Customers receive the same level of care. Years ago, I managed a Barnes & Noble in Destin, Florida, in the Florida Panhandle, and whenever we had a tornado warning or a hurricane was coming through, people sought comfort in the bookstore. Our café would be packed with people who needed somewhere familiar to stay, somewhere they could literally weather the storm.

There's no real way to explain these deep connections

beyond the subconscious phenomenon of relating books to family. When we're little, we read picture books, and little board books, and Dr. Seuss. We grow up, and we make connections between the story times and the books to our families. When someone loses their job, or they're coping with a miscarriage, or a family member is diagnosed with Alzheimer's, anything like that, booksellers are so often the ones who take a moment to listen, to comfort them.

It makes me emotional just thinking about it.

In our minds, it's *Oh yeah. The bookstore, I love going there.* It's possible we don't really understand why we love going there. We just know that we do.

Lynn Greene

Lynn Greene is the general manager at Books-A-Million in Vero Beach, Florida.

It's closing time when a guy comes into the store and says, "Hi, my name's Brad Meltzer. I was wondering if I could sign my book."

"Sure," I say, "as long as you sign the first one to Lynn."

We've been friends ever since.

He stops in on book tour every year—except for when he got stuck in Cleveland.

"Lynn," he says when he calls me, "I'm not going to make it to the store. I feel so bad."

"That's okay, Brad," I say. "I understand. It's the weather, so you have nothing to do with it."

My husband and I decide to drive the two hours down to Boca Raton for a signing Brad's doing there later.

"I can't believe you drove all this way," Brad says. "Now you can spend some time with my family."

So we hang out with his dad and his kids, and I have Brad autograph my grandson's thirteen books from the I Am series, along with my new hardcover.

I've been with Books-A-Million for thirteen years now—and before that, I was with Waldenbooks in this same space—so I've been selling books in this one location for twenty-five years.

Vero Beach is in Indian River County, Florida, which has blown up with people moving down permanently from up north or California or Illinois or Kentucky. We moved down ourselves from New Jersey about forty-four years ago.

I've developed friendships with customers over the years. I've watched kids grow up from babies to college kids—which is very disturbing because it means I'm old, but it's fun.

A girl comes in one day and tells me she just got accepted to college.

"Wait a minute!" I exclaim. "I can still remember the day you came in before you started kindergarten!"

A lot of people come to Vero Beach seasonally too.

"Oh, you're here." A lady from England recognizes me. "We were here last year," she says, "and you gave me a really good book to read. What do you suggest this year?"

"What book did I tell you about last year?" I ask. I find her another title. "Oh, this is a great book. You'll love it."

"You were right," she says when she comes back in. "I couldn't believe how good it is."

Other times, people walk in saying, "Tell me what to read."

"What have you read lately?" I ask. And a lot of people say, "Well, I just got done reading this..."

"Did you like it?"

"Not really."

"Okay, well then, I'm going to pick a different kind of book for you."

A mother comes in. Her teenage son has an assignment where he has to read a nonfiction or a fiction book. I recommend an adult title, James Patterson's *Kiss the Girls,* but with a warning.

"Now," I say, "there's a little bit of sex in it. I'm telling you because you're the mom and you're buying this book."

"I'm okay with it," she says. She later makes sure to tell me that her son enjoyed the book, and he did well on his report.

As the Alex Cross series progresses, I get an advance copy of *Roses Are Red* packaged with a silk rose. Awhile later, after the book comes out, a guy comes in and wants to buy it as a Valentine's Day gift for his girlfriend.

"Go buy a red silk rose, wrap the book, and put the flower on top of the package," I recommend.

"Oh, that's a cool idea."

My three loves are people, books, and—after twenty-five years spent first in banking—dealing with money. Bookselling combines the best of all three.

When I recommend a book, I don't think of it as selling.

A district manager of mine once said, "Oh, I can sell any book in this store to anybody."

"Not in this store," I said, "because I want them to come back. I'm not going to sell them a book, just tell them about a book."

If you talk to people like they're friends as opposed to customers that you're trying to part from their money, it's a whole different environment.

When the senior vice president was in last year, he said, "I have to take pictures of your endcaps. You have the best endcaps in the whole company."

Well, we don't set them exactly like the company says. Company says, "Put these books on an endcap." I put mugs with it, I put bookmarks with it. I put all sorts of stuff that ties in with the books.

My store is also the only one in the whole company that does not have a money counter. During training, my district manager asks me why not.

"I can count better and faster than that thing," I say.

She asks, "So you don't want one?"

"No, because this is where I see how my staff counts money."

Customers certainly count their money.

One lady puts a book back because it's thirty-two cents cheaper on Amazon.

Now, if she'd had our discount card, she would have saved an additional $2.80. But no, she puts the book back.

I have a problem where I sort of tell it like it is. People come into the mall and see empty storefronts around. "This is the first time I've been to the mall in years," they tell me. "What happened?"

"It's the first time you've been to the mall in years," I reply. "It's as simple as that."

"You don't have to buy *everything* local," I say, "but if you want us to be here, buy every so often."

Diego Sandoval Hernandez

Diego Sandoval Hernandez is the supervising librarian for Jail and Prison Services at the Brooklyn Public Library in Brooklyn, New York.

Today marks my fifth year bringing library books to Rikers Island, one of the world's largest—and most violent—jails.

Although Rikers can be a dangerous place, the individuals incarcerated there are normal people, just like you and me. They are fathers, brothers, sons, neighbors, and friends. They have regular interests, like soccer, music, history, and science. They have family and friends who love them, and who miss them while they're in jail.

I'm the supervising librarian for Jail and Prison Services at the Brooklyn Public Library, and I lead an awesome team of correctional library workers. Rikers doesn't have what we call a "standing library." There's no room full of neatly lined bookshelves for people to visit. Instead, we keep our books in cramped closets, sometimes even resorting to using empty jail cells as storage spaces.

Most of the incarcerated individuals at Rikers haven't been convicted of a crime: four out of five people there are still waiting to go to trial. Some of the people there *have* been found guilty, but my coworkers and I believe that everyone deserves access to books and reference information, no matter what mistakes they've made. To us they are just library patrons.

Today, we'll be providing book cart services, rolling carts full of books from one housing area to another.

The housing areas—living spaces shared by around forty people—are almost always loud, chaotic, and tense. People there are anxious about upcoming trials, about how their families are coping. They are bored and restless due to being confined for months—or years—with extremely limited access to meaningful activity. They face daily humiliations, like not having privacy when they use the toilet or being chained at the ankles when they walk through the hallways. All these stresses gnaw at their mental health.

People at Rikers tell me that one of the things they miss most, apart from their families, is having peaceful, quiet alone time. That's part of why library services are so important to them: with the books they select from our cart, they can escape into their own worlds for a while.

The first patron I visit asks, "Do you have *The Autobiography of Malcolm X*?"

Like most of our patrons, this man is Black. People of color are a minority in America, but they make up the majority of the prison and jail population. Many of our patrons at Rikers have had brutally traumatic lives. They may have had parents affected by the crack epidemic, been sent to a juvenile prison when they were still in high school, or seen their friends killed by gang violence.

"I've read this one before," I tell him as I hand him a copy of the book. "You'll have to let me know what you think when I come back next week." He grins, says thanks, and heads back to his cell to start reading.

The next patron I visit is Latino. Spanish is the second-most-spoken language inside the jail, but I'm one of the only people in the correctional services library group who can speak Spanish fluently.

I explain our services in Spanish. The man relaxes, grateful to talk to someone who not only looks like him but can also speak his language. I know what a struggle that can be.

My dad was a Mexican diplomat, and I was eleven when we moved to the United States. I didn't speak English well, but I learned the language by going to the library, taking out the Harry Potter books, and reading them while listening to the audiobooks. It's alienating enough to live in a community where you don't speak the language; I can't imagine how much harder it must be when it includes people who dictate your life, like correctional officers and judges.

The patron doesn't want a book. Instead, he has a research question. Since the incarcerated at Rikers don't have access to the internet, we often do the research for them. Providing answers to research questions is another one of our core services. In library school, I learned how to sift through the web's plethora of unreliable sources to find credible information.

"I'll print out the information and mail it to you," I tell him.

I offer him one of our Spanish-language books. We don't have a lot of money to buy books, so we have to rely on donations, and our Spanish-language selection is slim.

People think my job is just carting around books to incarcerated people, but it's so much more than that.

Our TeleStory program connects family members with loved ones in custody at Rikers via teleconferencing equipment available at a limited number of New York Public Library locations. An incarcerated parent "televisiting" with their child can access library-provided toys, games, books, and arts and crafts.

One of my favorite programs is Daddy & Me, a workshop that gives incarcerated fathers the skills to encourage early literacy in their children. My team helps incarcerated fathers pick out books that their children would like. The fathers then spend weeks practicing reading the books aloud before making a recording. They put a lot of love into it. The audio recording each father makes is transferred to a USB, which is given to the kids, along with the printed book, during the jail's Family Day event. Getting all the way to Rikers can be tough for families, especially if one parent is left to provide economically for an entire family. If the family can't make it, we mail the book and the recording to them. Like all library services, this program operates at no cost to families.

This is what I love about public libraries, why I'm drawn to this work. Whether you're working in a branch or in jails, you can impact someone's life, see people's gratitude for the value you're providing.

I went to undergrad and library school in Montreal, Canada. I'm attracted to public libraries because I don't want to be limited to only working with university students. I really want to work with the general public. The New York Public Library comes to recruit at my library school, and talks about all the services they offer, such as the work they do with immigrants and incarcerated people.

They explain that there are three library systems in New York City: the New York Public Library system, which serves the Bronx, Staten Island, and Manhattan; Queens Public Library; and the Brooklyn Public Library. All three systems have outreach service departments and subdepartments that work with jails and prisons.

I go to work for the Brooklyn Public Library right out of school.

At the time, the outreach jail team is working with librarian volunteers, so I first start going into Rikers as a volunteer. Then I'm hired into the full-time supervisor position.

Rikers Island is supposed to be a short-term holding space, but of course that's not always the case. A lot of our patrons have been there for years and years.

When we aren't able to do in-person services during the

pandemic, we launch a mail-a-book program via tablets that are given to the people incarcerated at Rikers. It's such a basic service, just providing books, but the importance and the value that it has inside of jails are tenfold.

There's so much gratitude when the books start arriving. Message after message is sent to us saying, "We've been forgotten during this entire time and we're just so grateful that you guys are out there offering all these types of stuff."

When in-person services resume, on one of my first visits back, a very shy patron gets up the courage to ask me a question.

"Could you please bring me a Bible?"

"Of course," I tell him. I don't have one in my book cart, but I know I'll have it at the library. "I'll bring it to you next time," I assure him.

The next time I'm there, he approaches again.

"Do you have my Bible?"

"Yeah." I hand him the book. "Here's your Bible."

"Thank you so much." He gets emotional.

I ask another incarcerated person, who's around seventeen or eighteen years old, if he would like a book.

"I'm not a big reader," he says.

"What interests you?"

He shrugs.

I hand him a slim book on psychology that's been popular at the jail recently. His brow furrows in concentration as he reads the text printed on the back cover.

"How do you pronounce this word?" he asks.

"Which one?"

He points. As he asks more questions, it becomes clear that he has a very low reading level.

There's a lot of support available for people who want to get their GED, thanks to college volunteers. But those who don't have a high enough literacy level to take GED classes tend to fall through the cracks.

Knowing this patron needs some easier reading, I grab a selection for him from the bottom shelf of the cart—*Batman vs. Superman*.

His face lights up. "Wow! I didn't think you'd have comics."

"Of course!" I reply. "Reading should be fun. I'll bring you some more when I come back next week."

"Thanks, man! You really made my day."

Those are the moments that make it all worth it.

Lexi Beach

Lexi Beach is the founder and owner of the
Astoria Bookshop in Astoria, Queens, New York.

Why are there all these bookstores opening in Brooklyn?"
someone posts on Twitter. "Why doesn't anybody open
one in Queens? We read here too."

Central Astoria in Queens is about a twenty-minute walk
from the East River. It's a huge neighborhood, over 100,000
people. A neighborhood in need of a bookstore. There was one
store here, which sold a mix of new and remaindered books,
but it recently closed and there really isn't anything else in the
neighborhood.

I wonder what it would be like to own my own bookstore.

Working in books always seemed just right to me. The
irony is that I hated every book I was assigned in school, but
I was constantly reading for pleasure. So after college, I poke

around and decide to try working in publishing. I start as a temp at Simon & Schuster. I work in a few different departments and then get a full-time position in the sales department as a liaison between sales and publicity and bookstores.

The publishing industry is teeny-tiny. Everybody knows everybody or has worked with someone who's worked with the person I want to talk to. So, in early 2012, I start reaching out to friends of friends who own local bookstores. I start sending notes to women who own stores in Brooklyn that are models of what I think a bookstore can and should be in the modern era.

"Hey, we have a friend in common," I say to these bookstore owners, "and I want to talk to you about what you do. Do you have a minute?"

"Absolutely, yes," they all reply. "Come by and we'll chat." Booksellers are collegial people who tend to want to help each other out. The moment I say I want to be in this club, everyone immediately welcomes me. "Fantastic! You're one of us now."

These women all open up their businesses and their lives, share business plans and sales figures, and offer me part-time shifts at their stores. They give me so much insight and guidance. Other industries may not function this way, but booksellers happily share information and knowledge and experience, and bounce ideas off each other or steal ideas openly, tweaking them to meet their needs.

My goal is to have the store reflect and serve the neighborhood. When I first think, *Oh, here is a hole in the market. Is that a hole that I know how to fill?* I spend a lot of time looking up demographics for the neighborhood, then sending out surveys: *What is it that you want in a bookstore? What books do you like to buy?*

Queens is incredibly diverse, maybe the most diverse county on the planet. There are more languages spoken in Queens than anywhere else in the world. And Astoria often feels like the distillation of that. Some neighborhoods in Queens are a little bit more homogenous: Flushing is known for being a Chinese American community; Jackson Heights has a lot of Southeast Asians; Jamaica has more people of Caribbean descent. But Astoria has a little bit of everything. It's historically known as a Greek and Italian neighborhood. There's a big Spanish-speaking population, there's a big Bosnian community, there's an area of Steinway Street that's called Little Egypt.

My store—the Astoria Bookshop—opens in August 2013.

Even after all my hypothetical research, it takes a while to adjust to the needs of the physical customers coming through the door of my brick-and-mortar bookstore.

When I first open, I'm a one-woman operation. I desperately need help, but I want to make sure that I'll be able to consistently pay for a position before creating it.

My first hire after about a year is a customer who I see come in every few months, buy huge stacks of books, and then come in again a few months later. It turns out that she'd been a long-time Borders employee. Borders—which went bankrupt and closed its stores in September 2011—famously had really, really fantastic booksellers working for them. The timing works out perfectly for both of us, and we're still working together.

My favorite question to ask a potential new employee is "Okay, what are your favorite books? What can we add to the staff text table now? What are you going to be talking up to customers?"

Now I have a staff of six. Often these days, they suggest to me, "You know what would work better is, if we grew this section and moved this over here."

Every time a new person comes on staff, with their own history with books and their own favorites, our sales shift. It's fascinating to watch how directly an individual person can affect what we sell.

When I started the store, I had one shelf of poetry; now I have three or four shelves because people in this neighborhood buy poetry at a very rapid pace. We also sell a ton of romance. I had to get more in stock and offer a broader range of titles.

We have customers come in and say, "I have this really tricky person I need to buy something for." And that's always everyone's favorite customer to help because we get to solve the puzzle. We love the challenge. What's going to be the right gift for this person in your life who needs a book?

It might be an adult who's learning to read English or a relative who's not much of a reader. It might be a child, like the reluctant reader who came in recently carrying his whole piggy bank. He set it down at the register while he went to look at the books, trying to find the right one. He was willing to try. And that was just the sweetest thing.

One of the early pieces of research I do is find the local authors. When my store first opened, I'd find authors who live in Astoria by surprise. I'd be looking through catalogs and reading author bios, which mention living in New York but not in Queens. Whereas authors from Brooklyn are very noisy about living in Brooklyn.

I want to carry their books on my shelves, I want to have that relationship. A number of authors have moved to the neighborhood in the last few years. It's now gotten to the point where, when new books are coming out, I'm like, "Wait a minute, I have a customer with that name. Is that author the same person?"

Very often, it is.

Books about Queens are so much less common than books about Brooklyn or Manhattan. My customers really enjoy supporting their neighborhood authors and making their books bestsellers.

People love to read local.

Kelly Moore

Kelly Moore is an adult services librarian at a public library in the Dallas–Fort Worth area of northern Texas.

I want to make sure people keep getting books they want, books they like. I call it Book Joy, matching people with the books that will bring them the most happiness.

One day, a woman walking unsteadily with a cane comes into the library, looking for thrillers and spy books.

I quickly come up with a recommendation—Daniel Silva's Gabriel Allon series, about a master art restorer who's also an Israeli intelligence operative.

The series runs to more than twenty books, and the woman proceeds to devour every single one.

I get to know the woman. She has a computer at home but doesn't know how to log onto our website to request books.

Instead, she calls me. "Hey, I'm ready for some more books." I recommend books and put them aside, so they're ready when she arrives at our drive-up window.

One day, the woman comes in with her adult daughter and a laptop. I show them how to use the library catalog.

"I'll never forget the day I met you," the woman tells me. She smiles. "You have changed my life."

My first memory of reading is from around age four.

My father is a navy pilot, and we're living in Guam. Our home has a papasan chair, its bowl-shaped rattan frame covered by a thick, comfortable cushion. I curl up next to my mom as she reads me *Hop on Pop* and all the Dr. Seuss books.

Our middle school has its own library. I run my fingers across old Penguin Classics with their distinctive orange-and-blue covers. I start at the beginning of the alphabet and read through to the end.

In college I major in English. Reading becomes work. By the time I graduate, I'm burned out.

I don't want to read anything deep and serious. I only want to read light stuff.

That goes on for years, until one day on vacation in Colorado, I pick up *The Bean Trees* by Barbara Kingsolver. The story is filled with wonderful, memorable characters. I can't put it down.

It's such an incredible feeling, discovering a book as great as this.

The Bean Trees makes me fall in love with reading again.

This is what reading is supposed to be like.

I strongly believe that people need access to books that make them smile, even laugh out loud. Reading should never be a chore or a punishment.

When my boys are little, we go to the library together and I always let them choose. My older son likes fantasy, so he reads a lot of dragon books. My younger son isn't as much of a reader, but then he falls in love with, of all things, F. Scott Fitzgerald. "It's amazing," he says. "I can't believe how many things that I hear in the world are related back to things in literature." He's reading Fitzgerald novels not because he was forced to, but purely for the pleasure of the description and dialogue.

I go back to school at forty-seven and graduate with my master's degree in library science at age fifty.

My goal, my passion, is to become a special kind of matchmaker—matching people with books.

One regular patron is a snowbird who lives in Wisconsin during the summer and in the winter months comes down here to Texas. Every time she walks into the library, she opens her arms wide and says, "Feed me. Feed me books."

The older gentleman who approaches the counter isn't a regular patron. His name is Robert—a navy veteran in his seventies and an avid reader of political fiction.

I recommend a book by Tom Rosenstiel: *Shining City,* the first in a series about a Washington fixer hired to vet a Supreme Court nominee.

"What if I don't like it?" he asks.

"Use Nancy Pearl's formula," I say, explaining the blueprint that the famed librarian came up with over a decade ago. "She says you should give a book fifty pages. But if you're over the age of fifty, take your age and subtract it from a hundred. So, if you're seventy, give the book thirty pages. Life is too short to waste on reading a book you're not enjoying."

He checks out the book and soon returns, asking for the next in the series.

Then Robert stops coming to the library.

I find out that he's had surgery, a stent implanted to open clogged arteries in his brain. I get in touch with him.

"What book are you on in the series?" I ask.

"Number three."

"I'll put aside the next one for you."

Publishers often send librarians "advance reading copies," or ARCs—early, unfinalized prepublication editions. Librarians have big mouths. We love books and love to talk about them even more.

When the ARC for the newest book in Tom Rosenstiel's Rena and Brooks series comes in, I immediately think of Robert.

I give him the advance copy. Robert is so unbelievably happy to get an early read of this new book. I take a picture of him holding the ARC and send it to the author.

Public libraries are a public good. We try hard to stay relevant. We invest in technology. We invest in innovation. We are there to meet the needs of the community we're in. And we're staffed with some of the most naturally curious people out there. Come in and ask a question, and we joke that we'll chase you out into the parking lot when we finally find the answer, even if it's a week later.

I'm a very curious person myself. And I just don't give up. If I need to find something, I just keep going until I do.

Holly Strong

*Holly Strong is a store manager for Barnes &
Noble in Green Bay, Wisconsin.*

I 'll do anything you want," I tell the manager of my local
Barnes & Noble. "I will shelve, clean, do story time,
anything."

I've just graduated from college. I don't have a particular
career in mind, but I'm excited to do something in the book
industry.

Barnes & Noble feels like a great place to start. Growing
up, bookstores were always my home away from home. Places
where I could escape to learn or meet my friends. Places where
I always felt good about myself.

"I love your passion and enthusiasm," the manager says.
"Unfortunately, we're not hiring."

I give him my information anyway. "If something opens

up, please think of me. This is what I want to do. I can be flexible. I'll do whatever job you need. I love books."

"Do you have a favorite?"

I think about it for a moment.

"I'd have to say *Charlotte's Web*. To this day, I still have this vivid memory of reading it with my dad when I was about seven or eight. You know, the book deals with some sad, heavy topics, but I really bonded with my dad over it. That was when I realized, Wow, I *really* love reading."

Luckily, the manager takes a chance on me. "Would you take an entry-level job? It will be basic shelving and organizing. Nothing glamorous."

"Absolutely."

I develop a passion for bookselling. It deepens and grows stronger over the following months. I love the people I'm working with, the customers and the authors and the publishers. I'm hungry to learn everything I can.

There are a lot of jobs where you can work a register and have great customer service skills, but to really fit in this industry, you must love books. Bookselling isn't regular retail. It has a very different feel, and I love it.

One thing I quickly notice is that the number of teenagers looking for certain books in the young adult genre—what we call YA—is staggering.

I sense an opportunity.

"I'd like to start a YA book club," I tell my manager. "We have a lot of teenagers asking for books. They love books, but they seem so shy. I think it would be great for them to have a place to meet once a month to discuss books and make friends with other like-minded readers their own age."

"Go for it. I'll give you whatever you need."

Only three girls come to the first meeting. But with every month that passes, the number keeps growing. Now we have ten to twelve teenagers coming together monthly to discuss what they're reading.

From a sales perspective, it's really helpful to see what titles are resonating with these kids, but what I love—what brings me so much joy—is watching how passionate they are about reading. How they bond with each other, and how relaxed and happy and enthusiastic they are to be in each other's company and have a place where they feel accepted and heard.

I love seeing what an impact acceptance has had on these kids. Especially in an era when there's so much opportunity to sit looking at a screen, it's really important that teachers and parents and support systems nurture excitement about reading from a young age—before kids and their peers stop really caring.

I credit Ms. Sylvester, my tenth-grade English teacher, with rekindling my own childhood love of books, which had sort of died down in middle school, when it wasn't "cool" to be a reader. So many other teachers insisted, "This is what this book means," which didn't resonate with me. But Ms. Sylvester tapped into the idea that great books can be read in many different ways. They don't have to be the same for everybody.

Ever since then, all I want to do is learn all the ways a book can be experienced.

I'm grateful to social media like Instagram and TikTok,

which is encouraging teenagers—and even older readers—to try new books and is keeping them in the public conversation. So many customers walk in our doors saying, "I never read for fun until I saw this book on TikTok, but all of a sudden now I can't stop reading."

I try to keep up with the trends, so I can make sure we have whatever the customer is looking for—or so that I can offer great suggestions. "Let me feed you all these other books that you're missing out on. Let me give you all these experiences, so that you keep that newfound passion."

A bookstore has many powers. If you want an escape from your life with a thrilling tale of adventure or romance or a good murder mystery, you'll find it. If you want to learn something or locate information on a particular subject, you can find that too. Whatever you want or require, a bookstore will almost always have something to meet your needs.

It can also be an incredibly healing place.

The high schooler standing by our staff recommendation shelves is alone and looks upset.

I can tell that something is weighing on the teen's mind.

Having done this a long time now, I have a pretty good sense of when it's best to go up and ask customers directly what they need—and when to wait for them to seek out one of us.

I decide to approach. I move closer and put myself in the high schooler's line of vision.

The poor kid has clearly been crying. They look so lost.

"Are you okay?" I ask. "Can I help you with anything?"

"I'm having a really bad day," the teen replies in a shaky voice. "I…well, I decided to tell my family some things about myself. About my…sexuality." Fresh tears break into sobs. "I'm so confused. I feel so alone."

Oh gosh, I think. *How do I fix this? How can I help?*

"Let's go over here and look at some books." I guide the teen over to the section of the bookstore containing books dealing with sexuality and gender.

"I won't say I know what you're going through," I explain, "but I can show you some books that have been highly recommended to me by others who have been in a similar situation."

Together, we look at some books. I have a lot of respect for how vulnerable this high school kid is being with me. "You may feel lost and confused right now," I say, "but there are many other people who have felt the same way you do now—others who've navigated their way through similar experiences and emotions. Your feelings are valid."

I emphasize, "I want you to leave here understanding that there are people in this world who will see your worth and your value. You are not alone."

"Thank you," the teen says a little while later, collecting a stack of books from the front counter. "I feel so much better."

To be that support for a complete stranger, who doesn't feel like a stranger anymore—that's the power and magic of my job.

Meg Wasmer

Meg Wasmer is a co-owner of Copper Dog Books in Beverly, Massachusetts.

I'm waiting in the grocery store checkout line with my mother. To pass the time, I look through the book racks near the register. Among a selection of adult paperbacks, I see a book called *Jedi Search* by Kevin J. Anderson.

I'm nine years old.

I *love* Star Wars.

I grab the book. *Jedi Search* is clearly written for grown-ups—no pictures, small print, and lots of chapters, some containing words I don't know or fully understand.

I don't care. I *have* to read this book.

"Mom, can you please buy this? Please."

"Not now, honey, we have to—"

"Please, Mom. *Please*. I'm *begging* you."

We go back and forth for a bit. Somehow I manage to strong-arm my mother into buying the book for me.

Being a compulsive child, I read the book nine times in two months. *Jedi Search* ends in a way that suggests there are more Star Wars books out there.

I live in Ipswich, a historic coastal town located roughly an hour north of Boston, Massachusetts. We don't have any bookstores here, but there's a Lauriat's Booksellers a couple of towns over, at the Northshore Mall in Peabody. Whenever my parents go there to shop, I go with them and head straight to the science fiction section at Lauriat's, where I find more Star Wars novels.

A couple of years later, my English teacher, Mr. Holtz, looks at the book gripped in my hand and says, "What are you reading?"

"It's a Star Wars book."

He looks at the paperback. The spine is creased, the cover worn.

"How many times have you read it?" he asks.

"Twelve, I think."

"Would you like to read something that isn't related to Star Wars?"

"I guess."

He hands me a paperback, a science fiction novel called *Pawn of Prophecy* by David Eddings.

"It's my favorite," he says.

I love it.

I keep going back to the science fiction section at Lauriat's. Every time I go there, Bob, the manager of the store, recommends books for me. Sitting on the floor, looking over books as I wait for my parents to come get me when they're done shopping—that's where I fall in love with reading.

And with bookstores.

I own a bookstore now, Copper Dog Books, fifteen minutes from my hometown. After college sucked all the joy out of reading, I worked at video stores, game stores, and comic book shops before getting back to bookstores and regaining my love of reading.

A lot of parents bring their kids, who mostly gravitate to "media tie-ins"—books based on popular movies, TV shows, and video games. A mother comes in with her young son, who is around seven. They head to the back of the store, where the boy picks out a middle grade graphic novel based on the insanely popular video game *Minecraft*.

The boy's mother rolls her eyes and says, "Can you read something that's *not Minecraft*?"

Her words—her expression—can't penetrate his excitement.

Right on, I want to say to him. *Read what brings you joy.*

People look down on media tie-in books, believing they're not really considered "reading." But what people forget is how these books help kids get *excited* about reading. Then kids will meet people along the way who will steward them into readership—an English teacher sharing her favorite sci-fi novel. A family member who sees a book you might like and buys it for you.

Owning a business is exhausting. When I first bought

the store, I did what I'll call generalized bookselling—recommending books to customers, as well as some light ordering followed by restocking and store maintenance. Now, ten hours a week are devoted to being a data analyst, choosing and ordering books based on what my community likes—sci-fi, YA, romance. Genre books are my jam. I get a rush when someone comes in looking for books for specific interests, because I'm delighted to share my favorites, or hand them the book that just matches perfectly. It's the best.

Three miles away, there's another indie bookstore, the Book Shop of Beverly Farms. We're both doing well, thriving by making sure that people have good books. But we cater to very, very different markets. Their top seller is poetry. Ours is genre fiction.

Their customers rarely come here, and ours rarely go there, but like neighbors who lend each other cups of sugar, we help each other out. The algorithm can't do that for you.

A customer comes into the store and says, "I've got a neurodivergent teenage son with ADHD. Could you recommend a book? Preferably sci-fi?"

"I love sci-fi and fantasy!" I say. "I've got the *perfect* books for your son—the Murderbot Diaries, a series by Martha Wells. It's won all sorts of prestigious awards. He'll love it."

Another customer comes into the store. "I'm looking for a book. I don't know the title, but the cover is blue."

"What's it about? Do you know?"

"Dystopian, I'm pretty sure. And it's long, about nine hundred pages."

I show her *The Passage* by Justin Cronin.

"Yes!" the woman practically screams. *"I can't believe you found it!"*

There is no higher high than winning the "cover is blue" contest.

Mike Bursaw

Mike Bursaw is the owner of Mystery Mike's in Carmel, Indiana.

Treasure hunting is my gig.

I'm in Albuquerque, New Mexico, for the Left Coast Crime conference in 2022, an annual event by and for mystery fans begun in San Francisco in 1991. My good friend George Easter, editor of *Deadly Pleasures Mystery Magazine,* discovers over lunch that the Albuquerque and Bernalillo County Library is holding a book sale.

I can't resist.

Public library sales and estate sales are prime opportunities to rummage for the kind of hard-to-find, out-of-print, and rare books that I resell through my company, Mystery Mike's.

I'm always on the lookout for collectible first editions or signed copies, especially any book by early pioneers of the genre, guys like Raymond Chandler and Dashiell Hammett, who wrote hard-boiled detective classics like *The Big Sleep* and *The Maltese Falcon*. Or Ross Macdonald, a California author whose novels featuring the detective Lew Archer helped elevate mysteries from pulp into literature, and John D. MacDonald, best known for his Travis McGee PI novels.

Elmore Leonard, an icon best known for crime thrillers like *Out of Sight* and *Get Shorty*, began his career in the 1950s and 1960s writing Westerns. I once bought one of his early Westerns in hardcover for about thirty dollars. A rare find, since hardcover print runs for Westerns of that era were pretty limited. Even better, when Elmore Leonard and I were at a conference in 2000, I had him sign the book for me.

Last year, I sold that one for $3,750.

To find really good copies of popular authors' early books, especially signed and in great condition, is quite unusual.

But not impossible.

That's what makes treasure hunting so much fun.

At the Albuquerque Library sale, I luck upon a mint first edition of *The Terminal List,* bestselling thriller writer Jack Carr's first novel.

I know Jack. And Amazon has recently adapted this book into a Prime Video series starring Chris Pratt.

I buy the book for a buck, get Jack to sign it, then sell it for $695.

I've been in the book business since I was fifteen.

That summer, a wholesale book distributor called the Bookmen advertises in the newspaper, so I take the bus to downtown Minneapolis to answer the classified ad in person.

Ned Waldman, cofounder of the Bookmen with Norton Stillman, looks over my job application.

"You're not in college?" Ned asks. "We only hire college kids."

"Try me out for two or three weeks," I say. "If you don't like me, just send me away. No harm, no foul."

The Bookmen is a small company that sells kids' books, mysteries, religious books—you name it, they carry it. I start out sweeping the floors, cleaning the bathrooms, and stocking the shelves. When I graduate high school, I go to work for them full-time. I meet salespeople and authors, learn so much about the book business, and buy books at a discount.

What's not to love?

Work is my college. It's like getting a focused course on books and how to run a business. It's a never-ending process. I'm always learning.

Every business boils down to having the ability to assist others. Can you help grow and build a company? Can you make money? Can you provide jobs and a great place for people to work?

Along the way, I leave the Bookmen to work for other companies, in other businesses. I'm constantly on the lookout for opportunities, and in 1986 I come up with the idea to launch Mystery Mike's.

In the beginning, we sell new books at Mystery Mike's. But we can't compete with Amazon and Barnes & Noble. So we pivot. What can Mystery Mike's do to keep the business growing? What can we do to be different—and survive?

We target a different niche.

Mystery Mike's is going to be one of the best resellers of fine books, whether they're ten bucks or $3,000.

I travel all over the United States to examine collections comprising hundreds and, in some cases, up to a couple thousand books. I get a lot of calls because I'm known as an honest guy who gives a good, fair price. In business, relationships are everything, and I want my customers to be happy.

In 2013, I get the most unusual call of my treasure-hunting career.

"When my mother died," says the woman on the other end of the line, "my father devoted himself to collecting books. He took excellent care of them right up until the day he passed away."

"How many books are you looking to sell?"

"Roughly fifty thousand."

I'm speechless. A private collection of this size is practically unheard of.

"Would you be interested?" the woman asks.

"Let me make some calls," I tell her. But of course I'll have to go and look. You never know what you might find.

This is going to be a *big* job.

I can't sort through this collection alone, so my two friends and fellow crime novel collectors Mike Dillman and George Easter accompany me to Madison, Wisconsin.

My first thought when the woman described the size of her father's collection was that the man might've been a hoarder. When we arrive at the deceased man's home, I'm thinking we're going to find rooms packed with musty, moisture-damaged books with loose bindings, mildew-stained pages, and little to no value.

I'm surprised—and relieved—to find that the books appear to be in fantastic condition, thanks in part to the several dehumidifiers the owner set up all over his house.

The collection has been meticulously cared for, and it's extremely organized. The owner listed each book, and its location in the house, in a notebook he left in the living room, where he spent his time reading. Too bad it's in Cyrillic, which I can't read. He'd been a Cyrillic professor at the University of Wisconsin. A stack of new books sits next to a chair, waiting to be shelved.

Now it's time to go treasure hunting.

For three days, we examine and box books. They're almost all in excellent condition. I find a lot of gems, such as the first mystery in Sue Grafton's Alphabet series, *"A" Is for Alibi*, which can be worth as much as $1,500.

I end up taking 7,000 books and partnering with Half Price Books, a national chain, which takes more than 40,000.

My friends and I are all over sixty, so I employ five guys

from the local high school hockey team to load the boxed books onto twenty-eight pallets—enough to fill a pair of semi-tractor-trailers.

News of my treasure spreads through mystery and book collector communities, who marvel at these rare, once-in-a-lifetime, mint-condition crime novels.

I've been a go-getter all my life. I'm almost seventy-three and pretty soon it will be time to hang up my book jersey. I want to take fewer book treasure-hunting trips and more vacations with my wife, visits to my adult kids.

But my reading hasn't slowed down.

The stack of waiting-to-be-read books on my nightstand towers as high as the Berlin Wall.

And I keep adding to it.

Erica Marks

Erica Marks is the youth services program director at the Cleveland Public Library in Cleveland, Ohio.

I like to dream big.

As the Cleveland Public Library's youth services program director, I want to give my community not only what it needs but what it deserves, which means always being on the lookout for upcoming books written by people of color.

I bring these authors and their stories to our Empowerment Events for young people. We have two, one called Man Up, CLE! and one called Girl Power. We invite students from our local schools to come to the library, we offer them meals, they get T-shirts, we have a DJ. Then they get to hear an author speak and they all get signed copies of the author's book. It's a day of fun.

Way before Jason Reynolds blows up and everybody's trying to get him, I invite him to our event after reading his amazing coming-of-age novel, *When I Was the Greatest,* which speaks to young urban teens and the heart of their daily struggles. When Reynolds comes, he speaks about his next book, *All American Boys,* with such genuine honesty that I can tell he connects on a real, deep level with the inner-city youth in the audience, especially the boys.

I host Malcom X's daughter Ilyasah Shabazz for a discussion of her memoir, *Growing Up X.* My goodness, it's like being in the presence of a queen. She's just so inspiring. The way she speaks, she just commands the room. The young ladies absolutely love her.

I book Angie Thomas, author of the award-winning novel *The Hate U Give,* about a sixteen-year-old girl who witnesses a fatal shooting. The victim is her best friend. The shooter is a police officer.

This story is, unfortunately, based on grim reality in the Black community. Authors like Thomas are taking our communal stories and putting them into the mainstream for the entire world so they can see, hear, and learn the hard truth about present-day struggles in America.

And it's working. The night of the event, so many people come to hear Thomas speak that we have to turn some of them away. Her powerful message and her stories—our stories—reach an audience of close to 600 people, some of whom drove from all over the Midwest just to hear her speak.

During the signing for Ibi Zoboi, the award-winning

Haitian American author of *American Street,* a young lady approaches me and says, "Listening to this author speak about who she is and where she came from—she was so honest. I could really relate to her." The students connect with Zoboi's authentic vibes and characters.

She holds up Zoboi's book and adds, "This is the first book in my life I've actually wanted to read."

Beyond organizing book and culture events, the youth services department is also a resource center for parents and educators, children and students, providing free lunches and after-school tutoring at all our branches.

I lead our summer reading challenge, which we call the Summer Lit League, and I help start the #CLEReads Young Adult Book Festival in partnership with Bailey Capelle of College Now Greater Cleveland and author Justin A. Reynolds.

Cleveland Book Week approaches, and I want to find a new author to introduce to the community. As I'm looking over publisher catalogs featuring new and upcoming titles, I stumble upon a debut young adult novel called *Beasts of Prey* by Ayana Gray.

What grabs me is the cover—a snake curling around palm-like leaves set against a black background. It's beautiful. Striking.

It gives me an idea. I reach out to the Cleveland Metroparks Zoo.

"I would like to host an event at the zoo," I say, after I explain who I am and why I'm calling. "I'll do an author interview, and then we'll do a book signing."

It's an unusual request, but they're up for it. "Where in the zoo would you like to have this event?"

"The rainforest."

Knowing that transportation is an issue for our community, we bus in middle school and high school students. It's an amazing event. I interview the author, and the students get their books signed right in the middle of the Metroparks rainforest. Have you ever heard of that being done?

It's just another magical way of bringing books to life. That's what I like to do.

At the beginning of the winter season, everyone is stuck indoors, depressed. Christmas is right around the corner.

"What can we do?" I ask my staff. "I don't want the holiday to pass without any celebration."

We toss around some ideas and come up with a program called Bright Lights, Reading Nights. I invite an author named Tiffany D. Jackson, whose first holiday picture book, *Santa in the City,* is coming out, to do a live reading in the outdoor Eastman Reading Garden on opening night.

I partner with Public Square, a public area in downtown Cleveland. Underneath the city's big Christmas tree strewn with holiday lights, we create a "story walk" where families can stroll around and read *Santa in the City*.

I've arranged for heating stations, but there's no need. It's a beautiful December night, nearly sixty degrees. We serve hot chocolate and popcorn and give away school supplies. It's magical.

An elderly lady comes up to me. She's in tears.

"Thank you," she says, grabbing my hand. "Thank you so much for having this amazing program."

She opens her mouth to say more, then instead gives me a big hug.

This is why I'm here. It's these moments that keep me going.

Nina Barrett

Nina Barrett is the owner of Bookends &
Beginnings in Evanston, Illinois, just north of
Chicago.

I was one of those New York kids who always wanted to go into book publishing. Shortly after graduating college, I work as an assistant editor at St. Martin's Press, and dream of discovering the next F. Scott Fitzgerald or Ernest Hemingway in the slush pile of unsolicited, unagented manuscripts. But, alas, the slush pile doesn't come through for me.

I next get a job as a reader for the Literary Guild, where part of my job is to read five to seven books a week and write reports on them. Boy, is that an education in the full scope of American book publishing.

As an English major at Yale specializing in nineteenth-century novels, I somehow got the impression that in order to get published, you had to write like Henry James or George Eliot. So it's eye-opening to see the range of everything actually being published, from very, very commercial bestsellers to very, very literary books. It's a real crash course.

In the old, ancient times when you couldn't order books online, there were two big mail-order clubs, the Literary Guild and the Book of the Month Club. Any book being published by any of the big publishing houses with any chance of landing on the bestseller lists comes across my desk so that I can read and report on whether it should become a Literary Guild selection. It might sound like a dream job, but reading and digesting that amount of information is pretty rigorous.

I see Margaret Atwood's *The Handmaid's Tale* in manuscript form. It absolutely blows me away, both as an incredible literary novel and one with incredible bestseller potential. I make a very strong recommendation for getting that book but am told that a Canadian literary author like Margaret Atwood doesn't have any real potential in the US market. In retrospect, I can say, Yes, I did call that one.

The experience leaves me a little bit restless. I'm also starting to think that I really want to be more on the writing side than on the publishing side. *You don't have to be Henry James,* I realize. *You can be anybody and still get a book published.* But I'm pretty sure I want to write nonfiction, so I decide to go to journalism school.

I apply to the Medill School of Journalism at Northwestern University in Evanston, just outside the city on Chicago's North Shore. My family has convinced me that New York is the literary and intellectual center of the universe, so taking this little Midwestern sojourn, so to speak, is a bit of a shock.

The way they teach at Medill, it's pretty much a boot camp. It's not theoretical. They just throw you out on the street and tell you to come back with a story by deadline. And so, for one of the very, very first stories I write in that program, I go into the heart of downtown Evanston and wander down an alleyway.

That's where I find a bookstore called Bookman's Alley, an antiquarian and rare-book store housed in an old garage. It would be anachronistic to say that it's like something out of Harry Potter, because Harry Potter didn't exist yet, but it looks like a store you would find in Diagon Alley.

An older gentleman presides over this magical environment, crazy stacks of books scattered over antique rugs, punctuated by a vintage set of golf clubs or an old saddle. I write a story about its incredible timeless bookstore feel. And lo and behold, that's the space that becomes my bookstore in 2014.

But thirty, almost thirty-five years ago, there isn't even a glimmer in my mind that I will one day own a bookstore.

Because I'd worked in book publishing and knew how to write a book proposal and who to submit it to, it's relatively easy for me to get a nonfiction book contract. So right after graduation, I start writing books—and I also start having children with my first husband. But fantasies about how wonderful life is as a writer don't mention that it can be very isolating. As is raising small children.

I start working in a local independent bookstore on Sundays. They basically pay me in books. I enjoy the social outreach so much that I keep that schedule for about fifteen years while I balance raising children with writing three books for Simon & Schuster. I really learn the bookselling business when I become an assistant manager, but by then Barnes & Noble and Borders stores are opening all over Chicago and it doesn't look like the independent bookstore is going to survive.

At that point, I decide to make a complete career change: I go to professional culinary school and get a chef's degree. *What's an even more precarious business than owning a bookstore?*

I combine my new culinary expertise with my journalism background and do food reporting for WBEZ, the NPR affiliate station in Chicago, creating a chef-centric radio food adventure series called *Fear of Frying*. Although doing the show doesn't necessarily pay the bills, it's a lot of fun and winds up winning the James Beard Award for radio two years in a row.

It's now 2013. More than thirty years after I wrote that story about the antiquarian store Bookman's Alley, I hear it's going out of business. And by this point, I feel there's definitely room to create a new bookstore outside the chain model. More of a college-town kind of bookstore, one that the Evanston community will really support.

The previous store liquidated, so we start from scratch with Bookends & Beginnings. Even so, the space is legendary in the book world. There's even a scene set in Bookman's Alley in the bestselling novel *The Time Traveler's Wife,* because the author, Audrey Niffenegger, loved it so much as a student. One of our very first Yelp reviews calls the store "a speakeasy for books, where you have to know the secret of its location, but then you can go in and get drunk on the books."

I make a point to preserve the rustic but cozy ambiance of Bookman's Alley, from antique rugs on the floor to antique furniture. One day I overhear two kids reading a book together on our little antique couch and commenting that they feel like they're in somebody's living room.

It's a lovely feeling, one that lasts for about a decade. Then a new landlord more than doubles our rent. When we can't raise the funds, we're served an eviction notice—two days before Thanksgiving and the official opening of the holiday shopping season.

Really smacks of Ebenezer Scrooge, doesn't it?

It's gutting. But the way the bookstore community and the town of Evanston immediately rally behind us is amazing. Within just a few months, we're able to move to another location only a few blocks away. The new space is light-filled and modern rather than dark and cozy, and I especially love the bright and colorful mural that my now grown sons—both professional artists—paint along one of our walls.

But the real blessing is when we open the door to welcome back all our regular customers, who arrive in droves. It really is about the books and the people, not the location.

The fantasy of owning a bookstore is imagining genteel days of reading something wonderful and drinking a cup of tea and enjoying conversations with the charming people who walk in, kind of like an independent movie set in Ireland.

The reality is a little different.

"Have you ever watched the *Firefly* series?" I ask my staff. The beloved cult TV show from the creator of *Buffy the Vampire Slayer* is a space opera about a motley crew of characters flying a big rust-bucket spaceship that's constantly having to be duct-taped together.

That's my vision, that I am the captain of a rust bucket with a crew of wonderful, quirky people who enjoy working in an independent bookstore. These are highly educated, very literate people who could do a lot of other things—but they gravitate here because they love books and bookstores so much.

It's a force field that bookstores have. And nothing could be further from the stereotype of a snooty bookstore staffer who only reads Nietzsche and who'll make you feel bad to ask for a popular book.

In my bookstore, we understand that books are for everybody.

Elaine Petrocelli

Elaine Petrocelli is the president and co-owner
of Book Passage, which has two locations: one
in the iconic San Francisco Ferry Building and
the other in Corte Madera, just north of San
Francisco, California.

Elaine, we need you on a red-eye for an early-morning presentation in New York."

I'm the assistant director of an educational nonprofit in California. I also have four children, and my travel schedule is taking a toll.

When I return, my husband and I go out for a nice dinner, just the two of us. Afterward, we wander into a nearby bookstore. I love bookstores. Have always harbored a fantasy about owning one. I'm walking the aisles, my eyes roving over the rows of shelves.

When I was growing up as an avid reader in Indianapolis, Indiana, the only bookstore in town wasn't a real bookstore, just a department store with a small book section. When I turned thirteen, I developed a rebellious habit—almost every Saturday morning, I'd tell my parents I was going out with friends. They had no idea I was actually taking the train from Indianapolis to Chicago. Alone.

My destination was always the same. First the art museum, then across the street to Kroch's and Brentano's Bookstore. Years later, I'm told that owner Carl Kroch had a reputation for being difficult—but he was the nicest man in the world to me. He let me sit and read until I caught the return train home in time for dinner.

My parents never found out. I finally confessed to my mother when she was ninety-five.

I smile at the memory. *Lying to my parents so I could secretly go to a bookstore. An act of rebellion? Maybe—for a nerd.*

Back in California, a bookseller smiles brightly and says, "Tell me what you're interested in."

"Well, I was thinking about owning a bookstore, but I don't know anything about it."

She takes me to the right section. "I know just the book. It's published by the American Booksellers Association."

On a whim, I decide to buy it. I start reading when I get home.

I keep turning the pages. When I'm finished, it's well after midnight. *This is it. This is my new career.*

I'm so excited, I can't sleep.

My husband is a lawyer. In the morning, while he is making breakfast for the family, I tell him I want to open a bookstore.

"I think that's a fantastic idea," he says.

"Really?"

"Everyone who comes into a bookstore wants to be there. Nobody who comes to see a lawyer wants to be there. Let's do it."

I'm glad he agrees. *Not that he could have stopped me.*

I find a space that's about 800 square feet, in a little place in Marin County called Larkspur. At first, I call the shop Lark Creek Books, but we quickly outgrow that spot after about a year and eventually decide that Book Passage is a better name. We've been in business now since 1976.

The book business can be tough.

I'm over eighty years old, probably the oldest bookseller working. I'm lucky to be healthy—and I give this great job a lot of that credit. This is the most interesting job anyone could ever have. It's the most maddening job, but it's the most interesting.

An eight-year-old boy runs into the store. He's really into the InvestiGators, a graphic novel series about alligators who investigate crimes. To hear him talking to one of our children's book experts, you'd think they were discussing the most recent Booker Prize winner.

"What's the next book I'm going to read?" he asks. "What do you have that I'm going to like?"

The Bay Area is full of great authors. I've lost count of the number of times Amy Tan's been in my bookstore, sitting in the fiction section, reading a book. It's always such a fabulous surprise to see her.

Years ago, Judy Greber, a local author and one of my favorite customers, calls to tell me about another local writer named Anne Lamott. Anne, she informs me, is a new mother and a relatively new author who's working as a waitress because of some business issue she's having with her publisher.

"Why don't you ask Anne to do a paid critique class?" Judy suggests. "You can give her a corner in the store."

I reach out to Anne Lamott. She's all for it.

I place a tiny ad in the local newspaper. The day it's published, fifty people sign up.

The class is a big hit.

Once a week for the next five years, Anne teaches in my store. While she's helping writers, I hold her baby. Those five years lead to Anne writing *Bird by Bird*, one of the greatest books on the craft of writing.

Judy calls me again. "You love mysteries. Why don't you start a mystery conference, help people learn to write mysteries and thrillers?"

Well, Judy was pretty smart about Anne Lamott. I guess I'll listen.

The mystery conference has gone on for thirty years

now. We keep it small, about a hundred students, and offer one-on-one teaching with mystery writers and editors. One student, Cara Black, goes on to become a bestselling mystery writer—and the cochair of our mystery conference.

Because of Anne, our store now has a department devoted to writing classes for different genres. Writing for children, travel writing. We host Friday pizza nights where young adult authors come talk to junior high and high school kids about writing. A screenwriter talks to the kids about *Save the Cat!*, a popular screenwriting book that breaks down the art of storytelling.

The kids are inspired. "What that screenwriter talked about," they tell each other. "*We* can do that."

Under the guidance of a wonderful advisor named Amanda Conrad, every kid takes a role—writing, illustrating, editing. A book designer volunteers professional services. We have books printed at the self-publishing service IngramSpark. We hold an author event. Parents and friends come out in droves. Grand-parents fly in from all over the country. I'm so proud I can't hold back my tears.

It's the best author event I've ever experienced.

Now the kids are on their fourth book. I know their love of books, writing, and cooperation is going to make these kids outstanding in their lives. Kids who like to hang out at book-stores are pretty special.

Book Passage hosts nearly 900 in-person events per year when the pandemic hits and we have to shut down. I write a letter to my customers saying we have to temporarily close the store.

I'm not feeling very positive about the future.

The next day, I get a call from a man who identifies himself as a frequent customer.

"My partner and I do online seminars where scientists and educators discuss new ideas," he tells me. "I want to offer our services to start a seminar I'm calling Conversations with Authors. We'll produce the events for you, free of charge."

I jump on the idea and start calling authors I know—Anne Lamott, Isabel Allende, and Khaled Hosseini, author of the international bestseller *The Kite Runner*—with worldwide fan bases. Ann Patchett, Dave Eggers, and Michael Connelly are also early participants. It's amazing, but not surprising, to see authors, readers, and industry organizations step forward, a supportive community that stretches far beyond the Bay Area. I can't think of any other business in the world where there's so much collegiality among people in the same business.

Many other customers also support us with generous donations. Authors too. With a pledge of $500,000, James Patterson helps launch the campaign #SaveIndieBookstores, saying, "I believe that books are essential. They make us kinder, more empathetic human beings. And they have the power to take us away—even momentarily—from feeling overwhelmed, anxious and scared."

The bookstore community is so compassionate. Another time, I get so sick that for months I'm unable to go to the store.

Isabel Allende, who's become a friend, volunteers to keep everything running smoothly.

One day our café barista doesn't show up for work. Isabel gets behind the counter to serve coffee to customers, make cappuccinos, everything.

"You're the best barista," a customer says. "Has anyone ever told you, you look like that famous author Isabel Allende?"

"Oh yes," Isabel replies. "I do hear that sometimes."

PART THREE

I can't imagine what people do
without books in their lives.

Miranda Berdahl

*Miranda Berdahl is the owner of Wind City
Books in Casper, Wyoming.*

I 'm a one-woman show.

Every day, I get up at 4:00 in the morning to lift weights
and do cardio. Exercise gets me energized for the long day
ahead, running Wind City Books. Then I'm off to drive my
fourteen-year-old daughter to jazz band practice by 6:45.

"Mom, I heard about a really cool book on BookTok."

BookTok is a very active community on TikTok, where
users make short videos recommending books. The platform
has become a major marketing force and is highly influential
with young adult women and Generation Z teenagers.

It's interesting to see some debut novels pop up and take
off out of the blue. "Where does this come from?" my staff and
I ask each other as we restock an unexpectedly popular title.

"Is it somebody's book club pick? Is this a BookTok thing?" The influence has been huge lately.

Fantasy is very, very, very popular with the market, as are romance novels. A lot of young teen girls come into the store to buy BookTok-recommended romance books. Which is great—though sometimes I do try to steer younger readers a little, if the book they're looking for doesn't seem quite right for them.

"Ah, maybe you don't want that book. You might like this other one instead," I suggest.

But I still want customers to have the freedom to choose. People read things for many different reasons. I don't think it's wise to make assumptions. I carry all kinds of books, so I'm probably going to have something in the store that's going to offend someone. I feel that any kind of book banning is very dangerous. It doesn't matter what's behind it.

Books have always been a part of my life. In my super-tiny hometown of Lusk, Wyoming, we used to boast about being the least-populated town in the least-populated county in the least-populated state. That was very much farm country, ranch country.

When I was growing up, my mother read to me and my younger sister. Then I discovered the library—and it was just never-ending books from there on. One that really impacted me, by a Hungarian author named Mária Szepes, is a novel from the 1940s called *The Red Lion,* about a man searching for the elixir of immortality. It's not well known, but it remains one of my favorite books to this day.

I fell in love with exploring the darker sides of human nature through books. I love horror. I'm drawn to the dark. I'm fascinated by human behavior and why we do what we do. When I was younger, I could finish an 800-plus-page Stephen King book in a day. It was easy. Now I'm a mom of two teenagers and the owner of a small business, so I need to be more strategic in carving out my reading time.

To keep growing my business, I need to read—and listen to—as many books as possible. And I make it my goal to read all genres. But I'm not one of those people who can dip in and out of multiple books. I'm a completist. I have to read one book at a time, just devote myself to it completely and totally. I really dive in and experience it.

The best I can do is to read one book at home and listen to one audiobook in the car. That's the most I can handle. These days I get through a lot more listening than I do reading because of life and having a family.

After I drop my daughter off at school, I turn on an audiobook called *Shad Hadid and the Alchemists of Alexandria* by George Jreije. It's a fantastic, funny, and magical middle grade story—by far my favorite children's pick of the year. I haven't encountered anything this good since Harry Potter.

Every day I'm reminded of the power of books, how they can be used to connect people and share ideas and topics. The power of books can be transcendent.

Nothing makes me happier than seeing the excitement on someone's face—children, especially—when they leave the store smiling and happy with books I've personally recommended.

I've always been the type of person with an inner drive to be the best, and to give my all. I'm very competitive, even with myself, and want to be at the top of whatever it is I'm doing. My drive and work ethic have granted me opportunities in leadership roles throughout my life—but I recognize that I'm a bit of a workaholic. I have an amazing, incredible manager and I've tried to be better about delegating to my staff because I overdo it a bit. But I also *like* being super busy, connecting with everyone who walks across our threshold. I want the love I feel for my customers to be reflected by all of us who work at the store.

This year, I've set myself a new goal: bring more popular authors to my store.

Wyoming has two *New York Times* bestselling, home-state authors, C. J. Box and Craig Johnson. Box is the author of the Joe Pickett and Dewell & Hoyt novels, both adapted into successful TV shows. Johnson wrote the Longmire mysteries, the basis for the Netflix original series *Longmire*. Those books fly off the shelves; I have trouble even keeping them in stock.

People, including publishers, have preconceived notions about Wyoming, that we can't get big bookstore turnouts. Fortunately, I have a relationship with both authors, and they make it a point to come to my store.

And they always draw big crowds. There's a beautiful array,

a beautiful collective of all types of people here in Casper. Really just some of the warmest, most loyal, incredible people.

I'm constantly working the phone, pitching my bookstore to my reps at the publishing houses. I tell them about C. J. Box, how we collaborate with a brewery here for an event that brings a lot of people out—and sells a lot of books. Beers and books and cowboy stuff.

I tell them about an event we did during the pandemic with Jeff Kinney, the author of the popular Diary of a Wimpy Kid books. We did an outdoor drive-through haunted-house setup for his last book. It was a huge success, one that wouldn't have been possible if it weren't for my amazing rep, who believed in me and recommended my store for this event.

I pick up the phone, determined. I won't stop, no matter what. I dance to the beat of my own drum. Always have, always will.

Dodie Ownes

*Dodie Ownes is an adult services librarian at
Denver Public Library in Denver, Colorado.*

I caught the librarian book bug as a junior in high school
doing an independent study on the sculptors Michelangelo
and Rodin.

None of the books I needed were available locally, so I had
to order them through interlibrary loan. Every time I got a call
telling me that one of my books had come in, I would borrow
my dad's Chevy Nomad station wagon and drive over to the
library. I was amazed that a seventeen-year-old high school kid
like me could access books from universities like Stanford and
Princeton.

"How do you get books from all over the country?" I asked
the librarians.

"We all share the books," they explained.

How cool.

My mom later reveals to me that she always assumed my treks to the library in high school were just excuses for me to sneak cigarettes. "We never expected you to actually become a librarian."

After college, I follow my now husband from the East Coast to the Midwest, where I work for a small florist magazine. My contact at the Ball Seed company tells me that she's what's called a special librarian.

I'm intrigued and decide to apply to library school. Nearby Rosary College is run by the Dominicans, and then there's this other little school called the University of Chicago.

Well, the University of Chicago's closer and it's bigger, I decide. *I'll apply there.*

I'm taken aback when I visit campus. *Holy crap. This is Gothic and everything. Nobel Prize winners go to the University of Chicago. They're never going to let me in here.*

I speak to a professor—his name, no joke, is Abe Bookstein—who tells me, "I don't think you're going to make it through the program."

Well, that does it. *I'm gonna show you, dude.*

I get into the program and take a campus job at the Joseph Regenstein Library. I thought I'd hate cataloging books. Turns out, I love it. It's like straightening out the world. Putting socks in the sock drawer, underwear in the underwear drawer. Everything goes where it belongs and makes it easy for other people to find.

Everyone assumes I'll go into cataloging after graduation,

but I get bored easily. "Oh, I know cataloging now. What else is there to do?"

I want to move to Colorado, so I give my husband a snowboard as a wedding present. I start applying for jobs out west, and the University of Colorado Denver, Auraria Campus, offers me a position as their systems librarian. The automated library system hires me away, and one of my jobs is to buy advertising. One day, my contact at *Library Journal,* the premier magazine for librarians and people who want to sell them stuff, says, "I'm moving from *Library Journal* to *Publishers Weekly.* Do you want to apply for my job?"

Well, remember that little magazine I worked for back in the day, *Florists' Review*? I figure, *I have magazine experience. I can do this.*

I hold that job for eight years, my longest-ever stint. When, eventually, I get bored, I freelance for a few years so I can spend more time with my kid.

After a while, I think, *You know what? I haven't worked in a public library. I want to do that.* I start with Douglas County Libraries, then later apply for a job at Denver Public Library in a department called Books and Borrowing. Out of 100 applicants, I'm the one hired.

I've been at DPL now for six and a half years, having a ball doing a little bit of everything on any given day. Our location, right across from the capitol and the county building, is always a hotbed of activity, even though only 3,000 of the 750,000 square feet in our building is currently open to the public while we're undergoing renovation.

We're in throwback style during construction, because although the staff can go up into the stacks to retrieve books, the customers can only go to the first floor. So it's like the old academic libraries, where you wrote down requests on a slip of paper and somebody then ran and got the books for you. It's amazing how much our patrons are willing to put up with to have a place to use a computer and get their books.

I'm also the cochair of the Colorado Association of Libraries Intellectual Freedom Committee. Here in Denver—a little liberal nugget in the middle of a big conservative circle—we get maybe one or two book challenges a year and they usually don't go any-where. But in Colorado Springs, Pikes Peak Library District has faced a ton of challenges. In Weld County, to the north of us, they fired a staffer for refusing to change the name of her book club for teens, even though the Woke Book Club is its name nationally. Every chapter in the country is called the Woke Book Club.

We all have the same mantra. You can decide what you and your kid read, but you can't decide what me and my kid read. Yet libraries are facing an array of protests—from program-ming challenges like protesting drag queen story hours, to dis-play challenges, to passive-aggressive shelving protests where some groups check out all the books they don't like and don't bring them back for months.

A hot topic within the American Library Association now is whether our libraries are really neutral. I'm in the camp that says, If we are going to carry *The Anarchist Cookbook,* then we also have to carry LGBTQ materials, and that also means that we have to carry something about Holocaust denial.

We don't discriminate against books—if somebody comes in wanting a book that they cannot get through interlibrary loan and we feel it fits in with our collection development process, we will buy it. But if that person is the only person who cares about it and nobody else checks the book out for another five years, it goes into our "consideration to weed" pile, because we can't keep books that people aren't reading. So a lot of times, these very single-minded books with a vendetta, they move out of the system all on their own.

I'm always thinking about what next to add to my varied career. I would love to dip in and dip out as a substitute librarian, maybe while also working in a bookstore, or even running a specialty store just for cookbooks.

"Your pen must be getting rusty," friends in the vendor business tell me. "You haven't written anything for us in a long time." I might sit down and write some articles on all I've seen and heard at the library.

For once, though, I'm not really restless to get out of here.

Angie Tally

*Angie Tally is the children's department manager
for the Country Bookshop in Southern Pines,
North Carolina.*

My plan is world domination.

Reading has always been a huge part of my life. That's
how I ended up getting hired at the Country Bookshop. Since
I was always in there buying books, one day Joan, the owner,
said, "You ever think about working here?"

I had a job at the time—one I was very happy with—so Joan
said, "Well, if that ever changes, let me know. Let's exchange
numbers."

I take a year off to be at home when I have my baby. The
following year, Joan calls me and says, "I'm ready to bring you
in. Are you ready for a job?"

That was twenty years ago.

I'm part-time when I start working at the Country Bookshop, but when the store expands and doubles its size, Joan has me take over responsibility for the whole children's section. Back then, young adult books were in a single spinner rack. Now, I joke with my coworkers, my world domination plan is for 50 percent of the store to be children's books.

It's possible. The number of children's books published every year—even ones for little kids—is constantly growing. When a kid comes in and says, "I've already read all the Harry Potters" or "I've never found a book I liked," I say, "Okay, come here. Let me show you what else is out there."

My life's mission is to get kids excited about books and reading.

Southern Pines is a super-interesting town that attracts a substantial off-season population, many of them retirees. If you live in New York, you come here for the winter. If you live in Florida, you come here for the summer. All our streets are named after different states. Fort Liberty, the biggest military installation in the country, is half an hour away. Some people, like me, grew up here and stayed here in Moore County. Others came for the horses. We have horse trails spanning 5,043 acres of publicly accessible, privately managed land. No bikes, cars, motorcycles, or baby strollers allowed. You can walk the trails, but it's not really encouraged.

Southern Pines is a very wealthy area, but the surrounding

counties aren't as fortunate. I start working to bring in these amazing, wonderful, award-winning *New York Times* bestselling authors to talk with students in the local schools. I work with school media specialists to put on fantastic presentations, with all the bells and whistles, to get these kids fired up to purchase an author's brand-new book, which the Country Bookshop then sells at a discounted price.

But only roughly 10 out of 200 kids buy it. Maybe some grandparents will buy the book for Christmas, or some moms will check the book out from the library. But most of the remaining kids, unfortunately, won't read the book at all, mainly for economic reasons.

Which is upsetting. Every student should have access to an author's new book.

So I expand my world domination plan. I decide that when an author comes to town to speak to classrooms, I'm going to find a way to provide books for *all* the kids.

I end up creating a nonprofit called Authors in Moore Schools, or AIMS. Armed with volunteers, our goal is to bring big-time authors—the best of the best—to different elementary and middle schools in Moore County. And now when an author visits, virtually or in person, AIMS gives a free copy of the author's book to an entire grade level.

Schools embrace the idea. Many reach out and say, "Well, if you're going to give us one grade level, we'll do a different grade level," and then they match funds, which automatically doubles how many kids come to an event, and how many kids take an author's book home with them.

AIMS is currently working with a big North Carolina–based bank called First Bank. They give me $30,000 and say, "Go spread the love." The First Bank Book Club is helping me bring award-winning children's authors to public elementary and middle schools throughout North and South Carolina.

We've replaced the cardboard playhouse in the back of the bookstore with one made of wood—the kind of big, sturdy playhouse you'd find in a family's backyard. Little kids take stacks of books to read on the stools or sit on the rug next to a giant Winnie-the-Pooh. They talk and play together in the playhouse.

I love seeing the bookstore being used as a community hub, a happy gathering place downtown. We celebrated seventy years in business in 2023, the last ten under the ownership of our local newspaper, *The Pilot*. Our store has a very fun vibe. The building is over a hundred years old and used to be a department store, with tin ceilings and wood floors that creak. Every bookcase was manufactured in a different decade. It gives the store character.

I love it when people walk through the front door, stop, and take a deep breath.

"It smells so good in here," they'll say.

It does. It smells like books, and it feels like home, and it's full of ideas and possibilities.

Joel Bangilan

*Joel Bangilan is the librarian at the Boniuk
Library in the Holocaust Museum Houston, in
Houston, Texas.*

My elementary school librarian seems to be the meanest person in the whole wide world, but she really knows what she's doing.

She teaches us how to use the library, how to find our books, and how to do the card catalog.

The librarian helps me understand that the Dewey Decimal System is more like an address than a classification system. That little number is going to tell you where a book is and it's also going to tell you how to locate relevant materials. Keep following along the road to find them.

"You're going to find where this book lives," she tells us, "so go to its address."

There's a code on the cards, and you have to learn a new language of storage and organization to figure out how to decode it. It isn't until years later that I realize this is probably one of my first linguistic experiences.

I'm a nearly native Texan. My family moved to Houston in 1972 when the oil industry (my father's field) and medicine (my mother's) were recruiting heavily from the Philippines, where I was born. I grew up here, went to local elementary and high schools, and graduated from the University of Houston with degrees in linguistics and Spanish literature.

My first job is as a children's specialist at the Houston Public Library. The branch where I work is in a mostly Spanish-speaking part of town. Some days we speak no English at all; some days we only speak a little bit of English here and there. Spending hours in a dual-language environment gets kids out of a corridor of misbehavior and onto a path of reading and learning and satisfying their own curiosity.

Can we say that we make a difference?

Certainly. I've since seen some of these kids turn into grown-ups...and even become fellow library professionals.

On my first day, I'm amazed to realize, *Gee, I've already used everything I learned from kindergarten all the way up to my final linguistics class within my first twenty-four hours of work. This is fantastic. I could do this for the rest of my life.*

That same day, I also do my first story time.

In the beginning, I aim to show kids that reading is fun by modeling my delivery on what I've seen on PBS, maybe *Sesame*

Street. Eventually, I develop my craft by joining the Houston Storytellers' Guild.

They really connect with many of our classic fairy tales, like "Cinderella" and "Little Red Riding Hood," the kind of stories that so many young children hear when they're first learning to speak. There are variations of these stories from across the globe. They're part of our evolution as a species, part of our humanity. They're culturally relevant and culturally inclusive. Almost everybody says, "Oh, my grandmama used to tell me that one" or "Oh, I've heard that one before," whether they're from Texas or New Zealand.

Wearing my linguist hat, I say to myself, "Oh, gosh, here's language acquisition in action."

After twenty-four years in the Houston and San Antonio public library systems, I see an interesting job listing for the Boniuk Library. The library is on the third floor of the Holocaust Museum in Houston, the fourth-largest museum of its kind in the country.

That seems like an exciting place to be, I think. It feels like a good transition.

It feels like something I can do for the rest of my life.

When I get the job, I start a story time at the Holocaust Museum.

"Story time's not serious enough to address something like the Holocaust," people say. But my attitude is, if we don't teach kids at an early age, just as they're starting to read, we miss out on the chance to create lifelong learners and thinkers. Even young children benefit from learning about things that are important to us here at the Holocaust Museum: sharing, community, cooperation, doing the right thing, being kind, and remembering the history of people who have gone on before us—so that the Holocaust never happens again.

That's the connection I see.

Among Holocaust museums, we are unique in having a lending library. Using my public library experience, I navigate the resources available to local visitors and those from across the country. Many researchers don't realize that their own public or university libraries have materials they can access either online or by interlibrary loan.

At the library, we work with survivors, many of whom are well into their nineties. Like Bill Orlin and Ruth Steinberg, two charming people who really enjoy being with kids and talking with school groups who are researching the Holocaust.

One of the jewels in our collection is our Holocaust survivor testimonies, video testimonies that were recorded in 1995. They've incredibly moving. I keep a lot of Kleenex in the viewing room. The moments of recognition are indescribable. Many of those survivors have since passed away, but that person comes back to life on-screen.

We're also building our collection of obituaries and digital obituaries. The memories of these people and the legacy of their experiences are being sustained, maintained, eternalized. They may be gone, but they're not forgotten.

To interest readers, from children to adults, in Holocaust literature, I immerse myself in the books I recommend. I didn't pay much attention to *The Diary of a Young Girl* by Anne Frank when I read it in eighth grade, so I reread it with fresh appreciation of the book as one of the ten most influential documents in the world.

There are many excellent children's books about this era of history, like Caldecott-winning author and illustrator Peter Sís's beautifully illustrated *Nicky & Vera*, about a British man who helped bring hundreds of Czech children to England to keep them safe during the war. Or Megan Hoyt's *Bartali's Bicycle*, about a champion cyclist who joined the Italian Resistance and hid messages in his bicycle tires. *The Length of a String* by Elissa Brent Weissman is a middle grade book about a Black American girl adopted into the family of a Holocaust survivor who finds the diary her grandmother kept at age twelve and gains a new understanding of her place in the world. And *This Light Between Us* by Andrew Fukuda is a great YA novel about a Japanese American boy in Washington who becomes pen pals with a Jewish girl in Paris, France, and their experiences during World War II.

Holocaust researchers are always making new discoveries and publishing their findings, often in digital formats. To supply the research needs of college-age students and even their professors, I work to expand our library's digital reach and learn a lot along the way about lesser-known subjects, like "What was happening in North Africa during the Holocaust and Nazi eras?" Our Eurocentric films and literature often seem to forget that this was a worldwide event. We have to remember that it happened all over.

In my own research, I've been tracing the effects of the US borders being closed to many Jews escaping Europe. Much has been written about Nazi war criminals fleeing to South America, but many countries there and in the Caribbean also accepted Jewish refugees, realizing, *This is just the right thing to do.* China and the Philippines were also parts of those rescue plans, and even Japan. Ironically, Japan was simultaneously fighting the Allied powers *and* rescuing European Jews.

It's not widely known that when Germany invaded Austria, Mexico was the only country in the world to say, "No, this is not right." In Austria, there stands a monument to Mexico's courage in protesting it.

Here in Houston, we have a street named Macario García Drive. In 1944, Sergeant Macario García was serving in the US Army's Fourth Infantry Division near Grosshau, Germany. His courageous solo attack on two German machine-gun clusters won him the Medal of Honor, the first Mexican national to receive America's highest military honor.

Too many stories of America's own Black and Hispanic military vets have failed to be captured. I recently contacted some colleagues in the Rio Grande Valley who've collected liberator and veteran papers and records and primary sources of local veterans. It took me a long time to put everything together. I realized, *Oh, here's one way that we can make a local connection and a cultural connection. We need to not leave this person out of our history.*

Part of our mission is to maintain and retain that legacy.

"Isn't it depressing, working at the Holocaust Museum?" some people ask.

I disagree. "Nelson Mandela said education is one of the best tools to change the world," I say. "I think our role here at the museum is to let people educate themselves, find out more, and elevate their awareness." Studying history helps us to recognize, and hopefully avoid, the same patterns.

My job isn't depressing—because our message is one of hope.

Roxanne Coady

*Roxanne Coady owns RJ Julia Booksellers in
Madison, Connecticut. She is also the host of the*
Just the Right Book *podcast on Lit Hub radio.*

Over the years, many people have asked me why my store is named RJ Julia. The short answer is that it's named after my father's mother. But I'll tell you the longer story.

My father is born and raised in Hungary. As World War II approaches, my recently widowed grandmother resolves that her son will finish high school—not easy at that place and time for a Jewish family without resources.

But my grandmother is determined. She makes the humbling decision to ask for help, accepting charity that will allow my dad to finish school, motivated by her commitment to his education and by her respect for and awe of books and learning.

Despite the odds, she accomplishes her dream: my dad

completes high school in 1942, launching his lifelong love of books and his insatiable desire to read.

But within a year, he is imprisoned in a labor camp, working as a minesweeper for the Germans. My grandmother is deported to Bergen-Belsen and killed.

My father's life is shaped by his mother's love, and by her loss.

Thanks to her fierce love and resilience, he survives and makes his way to America, where he opens a string of bakeries in New York, has six children, and realizes his version of the American dream.

Naturally, reading has always been a priority in our house. My immigrant parents and I learn English together, all of us reading phonetically from the Little Golden Books series, or my father and I sounding out articles from the *New York Post*. Of course, at first that means I think words like *know* are pronounced "k-now" and *weight* as "way-ga-hate." But we eventually figure it out. It doesn't matter—I discover early to get lost in the magic of the words, loving these stories with small creatures, like *The Poky Little Puppy,* or my favorite, *The Goat That Went to School*.

I want to read other books, and the logical place to find them is in the library. Unfortunately, my parents' history makes them nervous about filling out the forms necessary to get me a library card, so initially we stick with Little Golden Books and the *New York Post*.

A move to Connecticut when I'm ten changes my library fortunes. It's 1959 and I'm in the fifth grade. The library is right next to my school, Northwest-Jones Junior High School, in Hartford.

"Can I please get a library card?" I ask, hoping the years have softened my parents' worries at least a bit.

Although their fear of state-aided agencies never completely disappears, it's outweighed by the luxury of having access to all these books. I finally get the winning ticket: a library card!

The only books I've read up until this point are the Little Golden Books or Dick and Jane–type books in school. Although books like *Charlotte's Web* seem to be the next logical step, I'm hungry for *all* the books in the library, including adult books. I need even more permission for that, but my mother agrees to sign the form allowing me to read any book in the library—my idea of heaven.

I wander over to the adult section and scan the titles listed under NEW BOOKS. My attention lands on this huge hardcover book called *Exodus*, written by Leon Uris. It's a big, sprawling, epic story about Jews and war and romance. It reminds me of my parents, who are immigrants and refugees.

I check it out of the library.

I am mesmerized. *Exodus* is a story that combines history populated by vivid characters and, yes, sex. But what really blows my mind is how this story opens a wonderful gateway into reading, as well as its capacity to offer fascinating and sometimes terrifying insights into the world that exists beyond the walls of my classroom and home—life in the real world.

Fast-forward. I am happily married and living in New York City, enjoying a career at a big accounting firm as its national tax director, living the dream. But when I turn forty, something tugs at my heart. Maybe this is the time to follow my heart instead of my head.

My heart always comes back to books. Having them and being surrounded by them is, to me, one of life's most exquisite luxuries.

What would it be like to open a bookstore? Work for a publisher? What would it be like to become a publisher? Maybe even a writer?

Writing is out because I'm not a good writer. And I know nothing about publishing. The same is true for bookstores.

But I am a voracious reader, and my hobby is recommending books to friends.

That, ridiculously enough, gives me the confidence to start exploring the idea.

For a year, I visit bookstores across the country, interviewing owners and putting together a business plan and fiscal projections. Because we have a home in Branford, Connecticut, I'm leaning toward establishing a bookstore on the Connecticut shoreline.

I've done my due diligence. I feel confident that opening a bookstore is the right next step for me.

I tell my father.

"That sounds...expensive," he says. "And difficult."

"It will be, yes."

"And there's no guarantee that it will succeed."

He's right. The statistics on new businesses lasting more than a year are not encouraging.

"Why do you want to do this?" he asks. "You've worked so hard for this amazing, wonderful life you have in New York. You're living the American dream."

How do I describe to him the joyous feeling I get when I put the right book in the right hand? How do I explain that this small act has the potential to change someone's life? How do I explain how I want to create a business that makes a difference in the community? That I want to create a work environment that is satisfying and nourishing for my staff?

"This is something I need to do," I say.

"I don't think it's a good idea, but it's your decision."

I give my six months' notice to my firm.

Opening a bookstore is more expensive than I thought. I burn through a lot of personal capital.

It's very concerning. A real worry.

In the end, though, I design a beautiful store.

I drive my father over to the store before we open.

"I have a gift for you," I say.

"What are you talking about?"

I pull up to the bookstore. My dad looks at the big sign showing the store's name:

RJ JULIA

His mother's Hungarian name was Juliska—Julia in English.

"I wanted to honor your mother's dedication and love of learning," I say. "How it can change lives."

My father can't avoid being emotional. As much as he was opposed to me leaving my job, he's pretty damn happy to see a building named after his mother filled with books.

Now we are both happy. My grandmother's legacy is established and thriving. And I have followed my heart.

Thinking about the impact of being a child of immigrants brings to mind a time when my then high-school-aged son Edward and I visit the Tenement Museum on the Lower East Side, which offers guided tours through the re-created homes of the immigrants and migrants who lived there between the 1860s and 1980s.

"Mom, how do these apartments compare to the ones you, Granny, and Gramps lived in?"

I take him to the street where I grew up. Though the building has been torn down, I describe to him how the toilets were on the first floor—none of the apartments had their own bathrooms.

Edward's expression is a combination of confusion and shock.

"I don't understand," he says.

"What don't you understand?"

"The idea of you growing up in an apartment without its own toilet is . . ." He shakes his head. "It just doesn't seem possible." How could it be that our now privileged lives started off in a two-room tenement without a toilet?

He and I end up having this great conversation about whether today's immigrants will be able to have the same first-generation transformation that I was able to experience.

We both believe it's possible.

Books can make anything happen.

Cathy Jesson

Cathy Jesson and her daughter Caitlin are the co-owners of Black Bond Books, with locations throughout British Columbia, Canada.

We are a family of booksellers.

My mother, Madeline Neill, founds Black Bond Books in 1963, naming it after her grandmothers, Celia Black and Catherine Bond. Her first store is located in Brandon, Manitoba.

As a teenager, I need a job. I decide that I hate babysitting, so my mom offers me 25 cents an hour shelving books. Working at the bookshop feels good—so good that I've been a bookseller ever since.

My mother gets busier and so do I. In 1972, at age twenty-one, I take over managing the Brandon store while she opens a new store in White Rock, British Columbia. By 1977, I follow her to BC and open another location there. Working alongside other family members like my siblings, Vicky and Michael, Black Bond Books grows to have more than half a dozen locations.

Eventually, my mother decides to retire, so I buy the store and take over as president. In 2021, my daughter Caitlin, who by then has close to two decades of working in the family business, joins Black Bond Books as a full partner. Two years later, we're co-owners and celebrating sixty years of bookselling across our seven locations in British Columbia.

"This is my happy place," our customers constantly say.

We do everything we can to hold that feeling.

The perception that booksellers just sit around and read books is so not true!

As independent booksellers, we're responsible for every detail in our well-curated, well-rounded stores, which range in size from 1,500 square feet to our largest, almost 4,000 square feet.

Our top sellers are fiction, sci-fi/fantasy, and mystery—a favorite of mine because I'm always impressed that writers can still surprise me with new twists—but we give our managers and staff the ability to order whatever works best in their communities. Less top-down, and more what matters locally, especially in smaller places.

Our love of books is boundless, and so is our work ethic. We have to do everything—but our belief in what we do makes the not-so-fun stuff bearable. Even after all this time, I have customers come up to me in our stores and greet me by name. Then there's the nostalgia I feel seeing customers' kids, who are no longer kids, but who still love our stores.

I love the passion we share. We matter to them. And we can still surprise them.

We constantly hear, "You probably don't have this in stock." Then we rise to the challenge by having the book in store!

We see the excitement of teens. Teen readers are a huge and important growth area for us. It's a total misconception that they don't read, just because they're on their devices. They love books, and they love having physical books on their shelves.

Every book carries a memory. Many years ago, I attended the American Booksellers Association's launch for Judith Krantz's novel *Till We Meet Again*. The novel is set during World War II and features a lead character who learns to fly solo before her sixteenth birthday. A Spitfire airplane was on display in the ballroom and the whole space transformed into an airport hangar.

These were the days when money was no object for publisher promotion. *Sigh. Remember those days?*

It was a magical event. Still in my memory banks forty years later.

Today the magic continues with writers like Diana Gabaldon, bestselling author of the Outlander series. She's such an amazing, warm, caring person who never seems to change over the years despite her fame. Or authors like James Patterson. All that he does for booksellers and librarians really says, *This matters!*

So does the little girl in a rainbow tutu, sitting entranced on the floor of the store, reading a ballet book.

What could be better than that?

Maybe a new customer sharing this confidence:

"I haven't read in years."

We know just how to help.

We hand the long-lost reader a new book and the world opens up again.

Suzette Baker

Suzette Baker is a military veteran and former head librarian at the Kingsland Branch Library in Llano County, Texas.

I belong in a library. I've always belonged at the library.

Even as a child on my family's farm outside Corpus Christi, Texas, with half a dozen horses, cattle, sheep, and chickens, I didn't quite fit in. I was never a horse person. I'm not an outdoors person. I'm a book lover. Give me dragons and aliens in a good dystopian story and I'm happy.

Becoming a librarian feels like coming home.

The Kingsland Library is not just a place for books, it's the heart of the community. Kingsland is an unincorporated area with a population of about 7,000 people. There are no city, county, or state offices except for the library. If you want to apply for state benefits or find a job, the library is the only place with the free access you need. We teach our seniors how to use computers and help them set up email accounts so they can keep in touch with their doctors and grandchildren. In the summertime, people who can't afford air conditioning at home come to the library to get cool. Some come here to get water. We offer basic, necessary items—most of all, books and a friendly face.

Texas law states that a librarian for a county with fewer than 26,000 doesn't need an MLS. So even though I only have an associate's degree, not a master's degree in library science, I'm able to become a librarian in Llano County. And in 2021, when my boss is promoted to director of the Llano County Library System, I'm promoted to head librarian of the Kingsland Branch.

I'm also a military veteran, from a long line of veterans, and the mother of a son who served in Afghanistan. When you take the oath of service, you pledge to "support and defend the Constitution of the United States against all enemies, foreign and domestic." I'm a firm believer in the Bill of Rights.

What's happening now is worrying me.

It starts right after I take over as head librarian. A group comes forward with concerns about "pornography" in the library and sends the commissioner a list of sixty-one titles to be removed. My boss asks me to move the books.

I refuse.

The book list does not have any pornography on it. Several of the books deal with critical race theory and LGBTQ+ issues facing teenagers and young adults. Many are written by Black and Latino authors. There are even three DVDs on the list, all film adaptations of bestselling books: *The Cider House Rules; Me and Earl and the Dying Girl*; and *Boy Erased: A Memoir of Identity, Faith, and Family.*

"You can't put books behind the counter, and you can't take them off the shelf. That's censorship," I tell my boss. Censorship is a violation of freedom of speech, and freedom of speech is a basic American right.

I email her a link to the American Library Association's Office for Intellectual Freedom's YouTube webinar on censorship. The ALA is very succinct: a librarian "cannot act in loco parentis."

Good librarians know their collections, know their patrons, and can help direct reading choices, since one child may not read on the same level or have the same interests as another. But librarians are not here to parent your children. If you can't parent your children, that's on you. And every family's value system differs.

But children have a right to read, not just adults. Even the Supreme Court says so.

I don't move anything. I don't take anything off the shelf.

In January, the previous Llano County Library Advisory Board is dissolved, and a new library board is appointed. The majority of new members, some of whom don't even have library cards, heavily favor banning books.

I encourage the library director to approach the county

commissioners about hosting town hall meetings, and I ask that she talk to the county's lawyer about these issues. She refuses.

After I attend open meetings with fellow librarians and other concerned people from the community, the Llano County Library Advisory Board states that all future meetings will be held behind closed doors. The public can no longer attend—a violation of Texas's sunshine laws, which state that any committee with decision-making abilities cannot meet in private. I also receive notice from the library director stating that librarians cannot use personal or vacation time to attend open meetings.

These aren't isolated incidents. They're happening all over the country.

In February 2022, shortly after the Tennessee school board bans *Maus*, a graphic novel about the Holocaust, a pastor from the state livestreams a book-burning event on Facebook. A large crowd cheers as copies of books from the Harry Potter and Twilight series, among others, are tossed into a bonfire.

The incident in Tennessee inspires me to update our message board: *We put the "lit" in literature.* Inside, I create a display showing well-known banned books such as *To Kill a Mockingbird* and *Fahrenheit 451.*

I'm ordered to take down the display and remove it from the Kingsland Library Facebook page.

In early March, I'm terminated for "creating a disturbance, insubordination, violation of policies and failure to follow instructions."

I'm sad, but I have no regrets. The Texas Library Association conference in Fort Worth is the following month. *Well,* I decide, *you know what? I'm going.*

I pay for my own $750 ticket to go to the TLA as a non-library person, thinking, *I'm going to go in there, and nobody's going to know who I am, but I'm going to learn from the seminars, specifically those on freedom of speech and the violations and what's going on.*

But when I get there, everybody knows who I am. It's overwhelming, learning that I've played a part in the larger movement against censorship.

Roosevelt Weeks, director of libraries for the Austin Public Library, wants to meet me. Steve Potash, CEO of the digital distributor OverDrive—one of the systems canceled by our county for carrying what they called inappropriate books—hugs me and breaks down in tears.

I can't get over the recognition I'm receiving. I get to meet Nadine Strossen, author, law professor, and former president of the American Civil Liberties Union, and hear her phenomenal talk on freedom of speech.

Seven people in Llano County file a federal lawsuit against the county for violating their First and Fourteenth Amendment rights to free speech and due process.

In September 2022, the Llano County Commissioners try to close the Llano County Library and trade the building with the City of Llano, to turn it into a city hall. The proposal is rejected after public outcry over the closing.

On March 30, 2023, a year after I was dismissed, a federal judge orders in a preliminary injunction that the books pulled from the shelves in the Llano branch be returned within twenty-four hours. The books are returned.

On April 13, 2023, the commissioners hold a special meeting to potentially close all three Llano County libraries. When the community draws together to speak against this action, the commissioners vote to remove this item from the agenda.

People are looking at the situation. People are watching what's going on. Now more people need to stand up and make their voices heard.

Mary Elisabeth Anderson

*Mary Elisabeth Anderson is the co-manager
of the Books-A-Million in Kissimmee, Florida,
where she also runs the store's social media.*

As a twelve-year-old kid, I make a list of dream jobs.
Every time my family goes to Books-A-Million, I ask,
"How old do I have to be to work here? How old do I have to be
to work here?"

In 2017, my first year at Tennessee Tech, I apply for an open
seasonal position and dress up to meet the store managers.

They tell me I'm hired. Also "Just don't wear your heels
when you come to work."

"These are my interview shoes," I say.

On my first day, it feels as busy as Black Friday and they
throw me on the register. I have previous register experience,

but not with a computerized system. The cashier next to me says, "Ask Rocky if you need help."

I'm checking out books and Rocky's telling me, "Click this button, push this one." It's brutal, for sure. But I love it. I'm able to have conversations with parents and grandparents and I get to see what the community is reading. I don't leave the register except for my break, but by the end of the day I've picked it up quite easily.

The year before I start working at Books-A-Million, I take a Brit lit class at Roane State Community College. My favorite TV show at the time is *Shadowhunters,* based on Cassandra Clare's fantasy novels about a Brooklyn teenager with angelic blood, so I've also just started reading the series books for the first time.

I'm over at Books-A-Million doing my homework, since they have Wi-Fi, when a girl sits down in front of me and says, "I've seen you reading that Shadowhunters book. I'm Yvonne. You're in my Brit lit class." We end up talking for two hours. I do not finish my homework.

It was the first time I'd really spoken to Yvonne. When you're that age, you see everybody hanging out with everybody and you think that you want this huge group of friends. In reality, what you want is a small, close-knit group of good friends. A core group is going to be hard to find, but when you make friends like Yvonne, it is amazing.

Yvonne is the maid of honor at my wedding. She's a librarian now, and we go to book festivals together. We like to attend YALLFest, a young adult literature festival in Charleston. I've met so many authors there. I have a tote bag that I have them sign their names on. It's either that or carry around a suitcase full of their books, which does happen. I've seen wagons, I've seen suitcases. It's insane.

On long car rides, Yvonne and I listen to audiobooks together, which is a completely different experience from listening to an audiobook by yourself or reading a book in a book club, because you're experiencing it at the exact same time and having the same reactions.

I get my one and only speeding ticket on my way down to... I think it was Little Shop of Stories in Decatur, Georgia, outside of Atlanta, to see Rick Riordan speak and sign books from his Percy Jackson & the Olympians series. In school, those were the books I was reading in history class, under my desk.

Yvonne comes down here to Kissimmee, Florida, several times a year because she's got season passes to Disney World, which is twenty minutes down the road from here.

People from all over the world love Disney, and we get tourists from all over in the store, from Brazil and France, Germany and the UK, along with a host of Spanish-speaking customers. Half my team speaks Spanish, so they help me with the basics. I can give directions to the bathroom and to the shelves of Spanish-language books, and I do the closing announcement to send them on their way for the night. It's really cool that our Disney-adjacent store draws this cultural hodgepodge, especially during spring break.

Everyone wants a book to read on vacation. When people ask me for books that I'm not a fan of, I try to keep a straight face. "Yes, I can take you to this book," I say, while telling myself, *Don't tell them why you don't like it. They just want the book. They have their own reasons for it.*

On the other hand, I get overly excited when people bring some of my favorite books up to the register. I'm like, "Oh my gosh, I love this book. You're going to love it."

My favorite experience is being on the floor and having someone come in and say, "Look, I've got a ten-year-old boy. He doesn't like to read, but he's got to read for this summer reading program, and I have no clue what to get him that he's going to like."

I start asking questions like "Well, what does he watch on TV? What does he like to do? Does he play video games?" *Oftentimes the books that get those ten-year-old boys excited are the* Minecraft *books. We've got a ton of them, little novels that take place in the* Minecraft *world. So I like to start them there.* Or maybe it's *Fortnite,* or *Five Nights at Freddy's*—and then I'm able to narrow it down to a couple of books.

The best is when the parents come back in and they say, "It worked. He wants the next one."

Kids' fiction, any kind of books for kids, have gatekeepers. Kids are the intended readers, but they're not the ones making the purchases. It's grandparents, teachers, librarians, parents, older siblings. So you've got to be able to figure out how to make that book appealing to both the person buying it and the person who is supposed to be reading it.

And those gatekeepers are the ones that I most love to work with because (1) it's a challenge, (2) it is ten times more rewarding, and (3) I am a huge advocate for kids' literacy and getting kids excited about reading.

I could probably name my favorite books from each and every grade and I want kids to experience that same feeling, of realizing that books could teach me that the world isn't always the way that people think or understand.

Rick Riordan's books are ones I always pump up because they're super fast-paced but also have good world-building and get kids learning along the way. And that learning piece always gets the parents.

I want kids to know that reading isn't an isolating hobby. That there are other people out there who love books and they can join that community.

"Oh, people don't read anymore." I hear that all the time.

They are wrong. Reading is still a thing.

Suzanne Lucey

Suzanne Lucey and her husband own Page 158 Books in Wake Forest, North Carolina.

I love books. They're my sanity.

Growing up in Salem, Massachusetts, life for me and my siblings is constant chaos. My outlet is reading. I spend every hour I can at libraries and bookstores.

I have a big crush on a local boy named Dave, who frequents the same ice cream and pizza places I do—until he moves to Boca Raton, Florida.

I'm elated when I find out he's coming back to Massachusetts for college.

We start hanging out. We get married and have kids.

Fifteen years later, Dave is working for an investment company in Boston. The company gives him a choice: get laid off or take a job in either North Carolina or Texas.

We pick North Carolina because it's closer. Dave's company moves us to Wake Forest, a beautiful town with the hashtag #WhereQuaintMeetsCool. The Renaissance Centre for the Arts hosts a wide variety of musical acts, film festivals, and other cultural events. They're also hiring. The Centre is looking for someone interested in creating—and instructing—an arts program.

For two years back in Boston, I did a local community TV show called *Books and Authors* during which I'd interview authors for half an hour.

I enter the Renaissance Centre and tell them about my background. When I walk back outside, I have a new job: interviewing authors in town on book tour.

Our local bookstore carries new and old books and some crafts. The owner is a retired psychiatrist named Ken who orders the books I need for the book signings we hold after my author interviews.

One day, as I'm picking up books, I casually tell Ken, "I would love to own a bookstore."

It's an offhand remark. I think nothing of it.

I'm completely and utterly surprised when, three days later, Ken emails to ask if I want to buy his store.

My father is a third-generation business owner. He tells me I'm out of my mind. Everyone, he says, buys their books online now.

"I have a passion for books," I tell him. "My store is going to offer services that you can't get online."

"Like what?"

"Building a community. Making people feel welcome."

My father sighs. "I think you're crazy."

My husband is more supportive. Together, we sit down and talk with Ken. We do our due diligence, look over the numbers, and then negotiate a price.

I struggle to come up with a new name for the store. With six weeks until opening, I still don't have any ideas.

"Use your street number," a friend suggests.

"What?"

"Your street number is one-fifty-eight. Put *page* in front of it and *books* after it, and there's your store name."

Sold. My store will be called Page 158 Books.

Some people come into the store just to talk, which is fine because I encourage conversations. "Never just say, 'Hi, are you looking for something?'" I tell my staff. "I want you to make conversation. I want people to feel welcome here because if they do, they'll come back."

A man wearing a New York Yankees cap comes in and starts looking around. I tell him I'm from Boston and jokingly add, "Oh, and I hate the Yankees."

He doesn't grin or say anything. He's kind of stiff.

"Where are you from?" I ask.

He reluctantly engages in some small talk, then bursts into tears.

His wife, he tells me, died three weeks ago, and his brother-in-law died the week prior. He's just moved here from New Jersey and is by himself.

Oh my God, how alone must he feel?

I tell him what it was like when my family and I moved here, the feelings I had at the beginning, and then I listen to him talk. Making these personal connections is so important. It's not about selling books; it's about making a community.

We get a lot of interesting customers, especially between Thanksgiving and Christmastime.

One morning I answer the phone, and an older-sounding woman on the other end of the line says, "I'm told your store takes donated books."

"Yes, we do. Every quarter we have a used-book sale. All the profits go to a local charity."

"Wonderful. I want to get rid of all my husband's used porn books."

"I...well, I can't accept those," I say politely.

"Why not?"

Seriously? Where do I even start? "It's not something I want to sell, for reasons that I think are pretty obvious."

Another day at work, a Mercedes drives right up underneath the big sign for Page 158 Books, almost hitting our front door. The woman who steps out of the car is very well dressed. Regal.

She bursts into the store and says, "Is this the Bright Funeral Home?"

"No," I say, "the funeral home is right around the corner."

She looks around the bookstore, then back to me.

"Are you sure this isn't the right place?"

I nod. The woman, I'm assuming, is grief-stricken. It's the only explanation for her erratic driving and behavior.

"I'm sure. Let me give you directions."

Wake Forest is a community of haves and have-nots. One out of four kids here goes hungry every day. The statistics in some of the poorer counties are even worse.

And then there's the issue of literacy. There are so many smart kids who—because of COVID, home situations, whatever—don't get support when it comes to reading, which is a travesty because reading is crucial to everyday life.

I'm reminded of a story about the actor Sidney Poitier. When he came to the United States from the Bahamas as a young teen, he couldn't read. By age sixteen, he was working at a diner in New York, hoping to find work as an actor but unable to read scripts. A kind elderly waiter noticed him struggling, and patiently taught him every night after work.

That man helped transform Poitier's life.

Over my seven years in business, the connections, the friends I've made, the opportunities to help other people, the daily serious and goofy conversations—these experiences fill my soul, and that's a rare thing to find in any business. As are the comradery and friendships I've developed with other regional booksellers. We've organized community calendars together and assisted each other with author events. We're competitors, yes, but the attitude is always, "What can I do to help you?"

I love it.

One fellow bookstore owner knows I'm a big fan of Gloria Steinem. My friend was having a book signing at her store and invited me to meet the iconic writer, lecturer, political activist, and feminist organizer.

My friend introduces me. "Gloria, this is Suzanne. She owns Page 158 Books in Wake Forest."

"Page 158," Steinem says, curious. "What's the significance of that number?"

"It's my IQ," I say.

Steinem roars with laughter.

David Lucey

David Lucey and his wife own Page 158 Books in Wake Forest, North Carolina.

I'm working in my home office when I hear my wife, Suzanne, shriek from another room.

She runs into my office.

"He sent me an email," she says, her face flushed with excitement. "He wants to sell the bookstore to me."

"He" is Ken, the owner of the local bookstore in Wake Forest, North Carolina, where we've recently moved. It's been Sue's lifelong dream to own a bookstore.

I've also always loved books. To this day, one of my warmest memories is of my grandfather reading aloud to five-year-old me, turning the pages of *The Monster at the End of This Book,* a story narrated by Grover, the bright blue "cute, furry little monster" from *Sesame Street*. I still fondly remember my grandfather, raspy-voiced from terminal throat cancer, trying to sound like Grover as he read to me.

Owning a bookstore would be neat. Cool.

"We have to do this," Sue says.

We both have retail experience—Sue once worked for a mom-and-pop office supply store, and I managed a Staples back in Massachusetts—and, sure, we've visited hundreds of bookstores. But we've never been in the book business.

"We *have* to do this," Sue says again.

"Let's talk to Ken."

We sit down with him. He wants to sell us the store, his inventory, the shelving—everything. Suzanne and I go back home and run through the numbers to see if we can meet the purchase price without going into debt.

"I think we can do this," I tell my wife.

Getting the 1,200-square-foot store up and running for opening day is nerve-racking. My wife and I have picked out books we liked. We have some idea about what kids want to read because we have two kids of our own, but we won't know if we've correctly anticipated the needs of the community until local readers come in and start asking for new and favorite books.

Right now, it's a guessing game.

We open in July 2015, which turns out to be great timing. It's the same month as a major literary event. Earlier that year, HarperCollins announced they'd be releasing *Go Set a Watchman* by Pulitzer Prize–winning author Harper Lee on July 14. Lee's first and only other book, *To Kill a Mockingbird,* had come out in 1960 to more than fifty years of acclaim. Lee, now in her late eighties, explains that this new novel "isn't the sequel. This is the parent to *Mockingbird.*"

HarperCollins sets a first printing of two million copies. The book sells more than a million of them in its first week on sale. *Go Set a Watchman* brings a *lot* of people into our brand-new store.

As the store grows, we expand our offerings, especially book clubs—we have a total of eleven to date. Our book club members (mostly older women and a few men) tell us that the gatherings are a very important social activity for them. We get cards and letters thanking us. The widows are especially articulate. "This book club saved my life," one writes. "Now I have friends. A purposeful living."

I'm touched, even shocked, to find that we've created a lifeline.

Sue runs four of the clubs. Her tastes gravitate toward classics like *Don Quixote*—widely regarded as the first modern novel—and brand-new bestsellers like the ones endorsed by Oprah, Jenna Bush, or Reese Witherspoon in their own clubs.

When a couple of guys suggest reading science fiction, it's my turn to step forward to run a sci-fi book club, since I *love* sci-fi. The new club works out so well that my wife puts me in charge of another club, for nonfiction.

One night, I suggest that one of Sue's clubs read a book called *House of Leaves* by Mark Z. Danielewski. In essence, *House of Leaves* is about a fictional book that was made about a fictional movie about a fictional family that moves into a house they discover is bigger on the inside than it is on the outside. It's bizarre.

Really, really bizarre.

"It's too weird," Sue tells me. "No one in the book club wants to read it."

I suggest starting a book club called WTF Did I Just Read? just to see how many people are interested.

Surprisingly, I get a lot of interest.

WTF Did I Just Read? becomes my favorite book club, by far.

📖

Overall, having our bookstore has been a wonderful experience.

The sense of community here is incredible. Just incredible. Fun activities my wife and I started as community-builders—adult coloring nights or "baby's first visit to the bookstore"—have grown into so much more.

We've now known some of our customers for years. We knew parents before they had kids. People ask us if they can take photos for their family Christmas cards at the store. Kids who got books from us when they were young now want to take their prom and graduation pictures here.

"Thank you for doing this," people tell me, especially around the holidays.

My response is always the same. "It's my wife, not me. Thank her. She's the magic."

Kate Czyzewski

Kate Czyzewski is a bookseller, manager, and event coordinator at Thunder Road Books in Spring Lake, New Jersey.

In addition to being a kindergarten teacher in Howell, New Jersey, I also run a book blog called *The Salty Bookworm*. At a book event in 2019, I'm introduced to a woman named Elke Ridge.

In March 2021, I get a call from Elke. "A friend of mine is opening a bookstore in Spring Lake," she explains. "I immediately thought of you."

"I'm flattered," I tell her, "but I'm a teacher, not a bookseller." I've been teaching hybrid kindergarten—sometimes in person but mostly on Zoom—to my five-year-old students, my "nuggets," whom I love and adore.

"But would you be willing to meet with him? His name is Basil Iwanyk."

I google the name and learn that Basil is a successful film producer, born and raised right here in New Jersey. After moving to Los Angeles to make his mark in the film industry, he's produced tons of blockbuster movies—like *The Town, Sicario,* and the John Wick franchise—under the banner of his film production company, Thunder Road Films, named after Bruce Springsteen's classic song "Thunder Road."

Basil's a huge fan of the Boss, another New Jersey native. His bookstore is likewise going to be called Thunder Road Books.

I meet with Basil, who says his real mission—his true passion—is the art of storytelling. My passion is creating life-long readers.

"The downtown area here is beautiful," he says, "but I felt it was missing a bookstore. I want to bring a sense of community here to Spring Lake, a place where everyone can come together."

He wants me to work for him. Full-time.

"I have people who are really interested in being my manager," he says, "but they're not quite what I'm looking for. They don't have your passion for children's books and reading. I think you should be the manager."

"I don't know the first thing about managing a business."

"Well, I do. And you know children's books. How about the two of us figure it out together?"

I'm intrigued but don't know what to say. *Should I leave my teaching career? Should I stay? If I leave, I'm taking a big chance.*

I don't know what to do. I love children, I love teaching, and I love books.

Teaching has always been in my blood. My paternal grandmother, Mary, was a kindergarten teacher for over forty years. She instilled in me an intense work ethic as well as a love of learning and reading.

I still have the children's books my grandmother gave me. At home, I pick up my yellowed copy of *Danny and the Dinosaur,* open it, and smile when I see my own childlike handwriting in the middle of the book jacket. I'd written myself an important note: *Katherine, this is a good book, just remember.*

I also have a copy of *The Snowy Day* by Ezra Jack Keats. Still one of my favorites. Every time I read that book to my nuggets it transports me back to my kid self.

The main character, Peter, is a child of color. When I was younger, I assumed that the author, Keats, was Black too.

I was wrong. My grandmother told me that Keats was a Jewish immigrant who felt that people of color were missing from children's books and was adamant that all children deserved books that represented them.

I can feel my grandmother guiding me. She was a lifelong learner who was still reading right up until the week she passed away at age ninety-four.

I call Basil.

"Okay," I say. "Let's figure this out together."

Thunder Road Books opens in May 2021.

For the first six weeks, I'm finishing up the school year *and* working at the store. It's a steep learning curve for both Basil and me. At times, it's overwhelming.

We miss some things along the way, and we make plenty of mistakes. People are very gracious. They know we're new. Still, I put a lot of pressure on myself. I don't stop to say, *Hey, Kate, it's okay. You've only been doing this for a few months.*

On top of that, I'm a people pleaser who wants everyone to be happy. That's always been my way.

The lesson planner in me chooses books for our weekly Wednesday story time, popular with young moms and their kids. My friend Danielle brings her two-and-a-half-year-old son, Parker. Like a lot of toddlers, Parker loves running around, exploring. He has a hard time sitting still.

One day Danielle pulls me aside and says, "Parker is imitating us."

"What do you mean?"

"When we're at home, Parker goes to his bookshelf and takes out a book. He sits on the floor with it and turns the pages, pretending that he's"—she uses air quotes—"'reading.' It's the craziest thing."

"I'm not surprised. Story time is a great place to pick up early reading habits."

I never want to be preachy, but I'm a firm believer that taking kids to story time, where they can see other kids and adults reading, is such important work. Even though they can't "read" yet, when littles pick up books and explore them, they're developing the habits of lifelong readers.

I'll never stop being a teacher, and I still lead with that mindset at Thunder Road Books.

Jamie LaBarge

Jamie LaBarge is the senior inventory cluster support for Barnes & Noble bookstores in Kansas City, Kansas.

To be a bookseller, you have to play detective.

To do this job, you've got to be interested and curious. You've got to be willing to spend time with customers and to ask the questions that will help them find the books they're looking for.

Sometimes customers don't know what they want. Sometimes they're not sure. Sometimes they have all the wrong information, or only pieces of information, like the color of the cover, or part of the author's name, or a half-remembered title.

Not long ago, a woman came in looking for a particular book. "Now, I don't know what the book's called," she tells me. "But I *do* know that it's a book for people like him."

She points over her shoulder at a sullen young man, who looks to be somewhere between a teenager and a young adult. He doesn't seem happy to be here.

"I'm afraid I'll need a little more information," I say to the woman. "Can you elaborate?"

"That's my son."

"I mean about the book."

"Oh," his mother says. "It's something about your twenties… I don't know. Books you have to read. Something like that."

"A list of books you're supposed to read in your twenties?"

"No, no, no." She throws her hands up, exasperated. "To help him."

I look at her son. He stares down at the floor, embarrassed by his mother.

"Can you tell me anything about it?" I ask him.

He shakes his head, refusing to speak. It's clear that he's uninterested in whatever book it is that his mom wants him to read.

Her face suddenly brightens. She turns to me. "I remember! It was an article in the paper. An advice book for twentysome-things starting out in life!"

That makes sense. It's late spring, a month before grad-uation, a time when we sell a lot of books aimed at helping young adults starting off in their lives. I'm beginning to have a vague idea of what the book might be, but I can't recall the title either.

I walk over to the self-help section while the mother keeps talking to me about her son, who's still standing there silently.

Little by little, I start to clue in on the book she's probably thinking about.

I pluck off the shelf the latest edition of a book called *The Defining Decade: Why Your Twenties Matter—And How to Make the Most of Them Now* by Meg Jay and bring it over to them.

"That's it, that's the one I've been looking for!" the woman says, delighted. "Thank you, thank you, thank you!"

The son sighs.

I wonder if he's actually going to enjoy reading the book.

An older gentleman pulls his wallet out of his back pocket and hands me a little folded-up scrap of paper. "Do you have this book?" he asks.

I take the paper, which is soft with age, and carefully unfold it. It's from a magazine article featuring a title I don't recognize, so I look it up on our computer.

The book came out thirty years ago. It's long out of print.

"Sir, it says here that the book came out in 1993. How long have you been carrying this article in your wallet?"

"Oh, I bet I've had it in there all this time," he says, unbothered. "But since I'm here at the bookstore today, I figured it was a good time to ask."

I hand him back his magazine scrap and direct him to try the library or a used-book dealer.

Finding the right book for the right moment can make such an impact.

Some customers come in wanting the same books they loved as kids. They want to buy them for their own kids, or their grandchildren, and they jump for joy when you have exactly the thing that they're looking for.

Sometimes, though, it's not a joyous occasion.

I'm looking over inventory and notice that we're low on a book about grief. It prompts me to go to one of my colleagues.

"I have a theory," I say. "I don't want customers to have to ask for help in a moment when they're feeling vulnerable, embarrassed, or depressed. I want us to always have certain books—such as books about healing after loss—on hand. So customers can easily find them when they need them."

The other day, a grieving woman came up to me asking, "Do you have a book about how to deal with the death of a grandparent?"

"I do," I say. "I had such a hard time when my grandmother died. She was like a second mother to me."

I hand the woman a copy of *Healing After Loss*.

"I think this will help you," I say. "It really helped me."

The customer is crying. I'm also getting choked up, thinking about my grandmother.

"Gosh," I say, wiping my eyes. "I feel like I need to give you a hug."

"Would you?"

"Sure, of course I will."

A woman comes in with her daughter, who looks to be about eight years old.

"Ask her, ask her," the mom says, giving the little girl a gentle push in the small of her back.

The girl is nervous and won't talk to me, so her mom explains, "She's been saving her allowance money. She has a new baby brother. He just came two weeks ago, and she really wants to get him a book because she loves books and wants to read to him."

I take her to the children's section and say, "You can browse and pick out the perfect one."

As I'm ringing up another customer a short while later, the girl comes up to the register clutching a book. She's got her little fist full of dollars.

"Oh, what did you find for your baby brother?" I ask.

Without a word, she solemnly lays on the counter a copy of *Dragons Love Tacos*.

"This is what you've picked out?" I ask, swallowing a smile at the idea that such a serious girl has chosen such a fun, goofy book. "All right, looks great. Let's get it gift-wrapped for him."

Dena Heilik

*Dena Heilik is the head of Philbrick Hall, the
fiction and movie department at Parkway Central
Library, the main branch of the Free Library of
Philadelphia in Pennsylvania.*

I was always destined to fall in love with books. I didn't have
a choice. Both my parents are librarians.

They met, they went to library school together, they became
librarians together. I mean, I don't remember ever not loving
books and reading, but of course I run away from the idea of
becoming a librarian.

*Obviously, I'm not going to do exactly what my parents did.
That's just lame.*

So I get a degree in drama—though there aren't too many
good moneymaking jobs in the theater. Then about a year or so
after I graduate, I'm at a dinner party my parents are hosting for

a whole bunch of their librarian friends. Everyone around me is chatting, and suddenly I realize: *Oh no, I understand everything they're talking about, and it's actually interesting, dammit.*

The next day, I apply to library school.

I'm from Canada, but moving to a different country after library school seems like a really cool idea. My only criterion is that it be an English-speaking country where I can still get the internet and watch my favorite TV shows.

I don't get the job I apply to at a Swiss boarding school in the Alps. Or the job I apply to in England. But I do get one at a small liberal arts college in Sioux City, Iowa.

They have internet in Iowa, so I figure I'm all set. I'd never been to the United States before, but let's just say that Iowa was not the America I'd seen on television, either big city or white-picket-fence suburbia. I come from a city with a population of around a million people. Sioux City has less than a tenth of that, and it's clear pretty quickly that I am not cut out for small-city life.

A few years later, while at the American Library Association Midwinter Conference in Washington, DC, I go to the job placement center and put in my résumé. I end up getting a job offer at the New York Public Library in the Bronx and get a second interview with the University of Miami. The Free Library of Philadelphia is also interested in me.

I'm going to fly out, see what they're like, I decide.

Miami, even in February, is too hot and humid for me. The Bronx is too intimidating. But I fall in love with Philadelphia.

There's so much to do in Philly. There's so much to eat.

There's so much theater. There's so much history. The city is very walkable, and I love that the buildings are low enough so that you can see the sky. Plus, I'm Canadian—this is as warm a climate as I can handle.

I get a tour of the brand-new library branch about to open in Center City, near Chinatown. "We'd love for you to come here. What do you think?"

I think it's perfect. And I've been here ever since.

At first, I work in the branch library doing a little bit of everything. Then I get promoted to the Workplace at the central branch, where I help people find jobs and write their résumés. Unfortunately, I quickly learn that I have no interest in being a career counselor. I'm getting burned out.

"Dena, where do you want to go?" the head of public service asks me in 2005 during a major round of downsizing, when I take a voluntary demotion in lieu of a layoff.

"Since I actually have a drama degree and a background in theater, I'd like to go to the theater collection," I say.

He gives me a funny look and says, "I think you'd be perfect for the fiction department."

I shrug. "Okay."

He's right. I fall in love with the fiction department, like *in love*.

I'm mostly talking to people who are reading for pleasure, which is a completely different dynamic than helping someone with their homework or doing research or looking for jobs or anything like that. I get to see people who are talking about things they enjoy. And I get to be the person who facilitates their happiness, which is a really great feeling.

A little while later, my bosses come back to me. "Good news, Dena. Layoffs have been rescinded and we're reinstating you as supervisor!"

"Can't I just stay here?" I beg. "I didn't like what I was doing before. I love what I'm doing here."

They're confused. I don't think anyone had ever refused a re-promotion before. But they let me stay, and eventually I became the head of the department.

I've got five librarians in my department, and we take turns on the reference desk. I'm usually on the desk twice a day, which is a nice balance for me versus the behind-the-scenes work I do, including supervising over twenty people and overseeing the purchasing of all the books and DVDs for my department—and since we're the largest fiction and DVD department in the city, that's a lot of material.

I'm also in charge of the science fiction, fantasy, and romance sections, which makes me incredibly happy.

I've been amazingly lucky to be in the right place at the right time throughout my career. Even my drama degree comes in handy. Because let me tell you, whenever someone needs to step up and do some public speaking, or go on radio or TV, people say, *Oh, don't worry, Dena will do it.*

And they're right. Dena *will* do it.

The library is a great equalizer. Public libraries are open to everyone. And free. There aren't that many public spaces left where you can go without the expectation of spending money. We even have trained social workers available to help people who need it. As long as you follow basic rules of respect—rules that are the same for everybody—everyone is welcome.

There's one girl who comes in all the time, and I spend a year calling her Holly because I'm bad at names. She never corrects me, but I finally find out that her name is *not* Holly.

"I am so, so sorry," I apologize over and over.

"No, no, no, I like it," she insists. "I want you to keep calling me Holly."

She seems disappointed when I begin calling her by her real name. I think she liked having a secret library identity.

We have so many wonderful programs at the Free Library. At the Chinatown branch, we started a program called Beginners Teaching Beginners. The Chinese-speakers and English-speakers who met up to teach each other language skills went from individuals with absolutely no language in common to a great group of people who were able to communicate and socialize together. A newer program is the Edible Alphabet, which teaches people English through hands-on practical cooking. You don't even realize you're learning a language while you're following a recipe and cooking dinner. The program is run by our library's Culinary Literacy Center, which has a commercial kitchen that we use for culinary instruction.

We also have an instrument-lending library. We have a Business Resource and Innovation Center that can provide help with headshots and interviews, and assist with aspects of starting and running a business. One of our library branches has a "tiebrary" where you can borrow neckties for job interviews or formal occasions. Other branches lend out bird-watching backpack kits. The Richmond branch has a functioning beehive behind plexiglass. It's really cool to watch the bees come and go.

But even with all the great programs we have, it's still a pet peeve of mine not to highlight all the leisure-reading books available at the library! I can't imagine not reading for fun, but I know that many people view reading as work, which can cause them to resent it rather than enjoy it. Just reading for sheer pleasure, without expectation or judgment, is so important and rewarding. And having a place to read all the books you want—for free!—is a major part of what libraries offer.

Take a chance on something. We have so many great stories to share with you.

And remember: it's a library book. If you don't like it, return it and try something else!

PART FOUR

It doesn't matter *what* you like to read, as long as you love to read.

Mary Terry

Mary Terry works as an inventory commercial specialist at the Barnes & Noble in Beaumont, Texas.

I'm on my way to prepare for this afternoon's story time at the bookstore when a man stops me to ask for help. A young boy stands next to him.

"This is my son," the man says. "He's seven, and he's looking for a certain book. I'm pretty sure it's in the kids' department."

"You're in luck," I say brightly. "I'm Miss Mary, and children's books are my specialty."

This is the part of the job I love, getting kids hooked on books.

"Thing is," the father says, scratching his chin, "I don't think the title is real." He takes in a deep breath and sighs. "But we're going to ask anyway."

He looks at his son, who's grinning from ear to ear, and motions for the boy to make his request.

"Captain Underpants!" the boy says.

The dad rolls his eyes.

I ignore him and address the excited seven-year-old.

"Do you happen to know the rest of the title?" I ask.

"*The Attack of the Talking Toilets.*"

"Okay, I'm pretty sure we've got that one in stock," I say. "Follow me."

"Wait," the dad says. "This book is *real*?"

"Oh yes," I say. "The Captain Underpants books are a whole series! Each story follows the title character's rivals, from Talking Toilets to the Bionic Booger Boy to Sir Stinks-A-Lot. More than a dozen books in all, not including all the spin-offs. They're a big hit with kids your son's age."

The three of us stop in front of a shelf full of the author's books. I pluck out the title the boy was looking for and hand it to him.

"Ha!" the kid says to his father. "I *told* you it was real."

The boy is practically levitating. He can't stop smiling.

The father still can't believe that his son is this excited to read something so utterly ridiculous.

Getting kids to read, I want to tell the dad, is tricky. Especially boys. But boys tend to love silly humor and gross things. So if they can get their hands on a book they love, at an early age—it will get them into reading.

And a kid who reads is a kid who thinks.

It's raining outside during today's story time. Beaumont is located right near the Texas Gulf Coast, so we get a lot of stormy weather.

We hold story time in an area at the back of the store. For the really little kids, I read aloud to them from a small stage in front of a curtain. For the bigger kids who are learning to read, I read along with them at a little table with benches. It's so great, hearing the kids read out loud. They read a line, then look up at me for confirmation. Sometimes I'll nod my head and smile. Sometimes I'll say, "Yeah, you're doing it! Keep going. Keep going." They just light up, big smiles on their faces as they realize, *Oh, I can do this. I know how to do this now. I can read!*

Those moments are wonderful.

There's a good-sized crowd this afternoon, mostly toddlers and their parents glad to be out of the rain and excited for today's story time. The children are moving around on the small stage, occasionally freezing or jumping when a crash of thunder rumbles through the store.

I'll be reading a picture book from a series featuring the adventures of an adorable yellow puppy named Biscuit. Before the reading starts, I go backstage to greet a surprise visitor who's been booked for today, courtesy of the book's publisher: a six-foot-tall man dressed in a full Biscuit costume.

"When we go out, all you have to do is to stand next to me, with your back to the wall," I tell him.

"Yes ma'am," says Biscuit.

I pull back the small curtain. The kids are packed near the stage, some lingering on the stage when the parents start clapping, signaling to their children that story time is about to start.

I wave. "Hello, everyone! I'm so excited to read to you. And guess what? I've brought a very special guest with me today."

Biscuit follows me onto the stage and waves. Some of the littles, as I call the toddlers, are into it and cheer…but some of the others scream in terror at the sight of a gigantic six-foot-tall dog walking toward them.

One little girl runs away from the stage, crying, *"BIG DOG-GIE NO, BIG DOGGIE NO!"* A handful of equally terrified toddlers follow her and run into the waiting arms of their bemused parents.

Despite the pandemonium, I calmly take my seat and hold up today's book. "Look, everyone! It's *Biscuit and the Big Parade!"*

Just then, another crackle of thunder. The store lights blink on and off, and everyone screams. A little boy sitting next to me jumps to his feet.

"It's okay, everyone," I say in a gentle voice. "It's okay."

The boy grabs a chunk of my hair and clutches it to him like a cherished teddy bear. The boy's mother approaches the stage, saying, "Come here, Connell. Miss Mary doesn't need you right there."

Connell looks at me and smiles.

"I fine," he says, tightening his grip on my hair.

"Connell, come here," his mother pleads.

The boy moves away but won't let go my hair.

"You know what?" I say to Connell's mother. "Let's just leave him right where he is until he decides he doesn't need my hair anymore."

Despite everything—the six-foot-tall puppy, the lights flickering on and off, and Connell refusing to let go of my hair, even when we're passing out stickers to the kids—I manage to successfully make it through story time.

Afterward, as I'm cleaning up, another boy comes up to me, a four-year-old named Roy.

"Thank you for my sticker, Miss Mary," he says.

"You're very welcome, Roy."

"Don't go over by that table."

"What table?"

He points to one of our book tables a few feet away.

"Why not?" I ask. Dozens of potential concerns are suddenly flashing through my mind. "What's wrong with that table?"

"I pooted over there."

"Oh," I say, thankful it's nothing worse than a little fart. "Well, thank you for telling me, Roy."

"You're welcome," he says, and goes about his day.

Mara Zonderman

Mara Zonderman is the head of reference and adult services at the Westhampton Free Library in Westhampton Beach, New York.

My grandmother is 102 years old, and she's still a big reader. Books are usually the first thing she wants to talk to me about. "What are you reading?" she asks. When my kids and I visit, her first question is "Did you bring me any books?"

"Yes, I brought you books—and your great-grandsons," I always tease her.

My grandmother likes meaty stuff—mostly fiction, but she does read some nonfiction, and she's very open to reading about different cultures and different ideas. She loved *Mad Honey* by Jodi Picoult and enjoyed David Grann's *Killers of the Flower Moon*. I chose *Simon the Fiddler* by Paulette Jiles and *Washington Black* by Esi Edugyan for my book club based on her recommendation.

My patrons, and especially the members of my book club, love it when I say, "Oh, my grandmother recommended this book." I even make a bookmark to give patrons with some of her suggestions: *Mara's centenarian grandmother recommends...*

One of my earliest memories is of sitting with my parents while my dad reads to me. Although my parents divorce when I'm a kid, I'm fortunate to grow up within two very good library systems. We go to the library at least once a week.

My first job, during my senior year in high school, is in an independently owned bookstore. Later, I work at my college library as a reference assistant before going off to become a lawyer. Which is actually very common—there are a lot of former lawyers among librarians. After I get my law degree, I work as a lobbyist for nonprofits for a couple of years and am on the Readers' Advisory Committee of my local public library. I testify in front of our county commissioners about the need for library funding.

It makes me want to be more involved with libraries.

I decide to change careers and go back to school for my master's degree in library and information science. I really love the conversations around reading and books and literature that I get to have every day now. And thinking about ways to bring people into the library so that we can have more of those conversations!

A lot of people are simply not aware of what the public library can provide.

A woman comes in from the bank across the street. She's looking for a notary public, and the bank has referred her to us, since—among various other hats that I wear at the library—I'm also a notary public.

"I've lived in this community for thirty years," the woman says, "but I've never set foot in here."

Oh my God, don't tell me that, I think.

"What a lovely building," she continues, looking around. "I had no idea you offered so many services."

This is my chance. "Oh yes," I tell her. "Let me tell you about more of the things that we offer."

I can go on at length. "Did you know that you can download ebooks and audiobooks for free from your library? That you can come and learn a language for free through your library? We offer exercise classes that are way cheaper than the yoga studio down the street. We have cooking classes, book clubs…and that's just for adults!"

Another patron comes up to ask, "Hey, can you help me with this on my phone?"

I probably can. In addition to being book wizards—a term I love—we librarians also have to be technology gurus, since we get a lot of requests for help both navigating our digital services and assisting people with their phones and tablets. I'm pleased that people think to come to the library for help with their devices.

Sometimes I feel like a bartender because people love to come and tell me stories. It's not just "Hey, I'm looking for such and such a book." It's "Oh, my daughter-in-law recommended this book, and oh, let me show you a picture of my grandkids as long as we're talking about it. Did you know I used to be in real estate?" And eventually, I get their whole life stories, which is actually very useful in helping them find books they'll enjoy.

Before we're done, they probably ask, "By the way, can you print out something for me?" And of course we can do that too.

The trend of people checking out our ebooks and audiobooks online keeps going up. We saw a huge jump in those services during the pandemic, but I thought for sure that those numbers would start to come down when people were able to come back into the library. But they have not. The trend is definitely continuing to rise, even as circulation numbers for physical books and audiobooks stay fairly steady. Which is fantastic from my perspective. I don't care how you consume your books, whether you read them on paper, whether you read them on your Kindle or your phone or your tablet, or whether you are listening to them. I do all of the above, and it all counts, as far as I'm concerned. So I love it.

I'm the head of adult reference, but since I have school-age kids, I'm also the liaison with our local public school district. My role is to strengthen the relationship between the school and the library. There's a great nationwide program called PARP. (It used to stand for Parents As Reading Partners, but not everybody has a parent available, so now it stands for Pick a Reading Partner.) It's usually in March, when it's too gray and slushy to go outside, so we stay inside to read. Schools and libraries across the country do all kinds of creative things to encourage reading. In 2023, the elementary school librarian and I partner together for "Book Madness," essentially a March Madness tournament but with books.

When my younger son is in fourth grade, I oversee the third-through-fifth-grade bracket. I pick sixteen books that have won awards, or that I know my own kids have enjoyed, and every week in the month of March, I go into the school to talk to the kids about these books during their Monday lunch periods.

It's awesome. Each week I read the blurbs from the back of four different books, then ask the students, "So which book are you excited to read?" During the week, they vote on which book should move to the next round, so I also ask them, "Which book from last week did you read that you liked? Tell me what you thought about it. Were you excited about last week's winners?" The students are so engaged and so enthusiastic. It's just an absolute highlight of my week to go in and be that bridge between the kids and the library.

From the day my son started kindergarten, I was called "his mom," since that's how they knew me. But now they say, "You're the library lady!"

And after Mom, Library Lady is the best thing anybody can call me.

Katherine Walcott

Katherine Walcott is the general manager of
Coles, a subsidiary of Indigo Books and Music,
at Londonderry Mall in Edmonton, Alberta,
Canada.

Reports that books are dying out are greatly exaggerated.

I understand where the idea comes from. I've just finished my university degree when I start at Indigo, and after four years as an English literature major, even I don't read "for fun" anymore—I merely analyze and research and underline the same books that have been studied over and over again for decades. I no longer feel the magic of reading, and almost never step foot in bookstores.

But after graduating and getting married in 2019, I figure a temporary retail job in a bookstore will be a perfect fit while I figure out my next steps.

Some of my family members who aren't avid readers aren't so sure. They ask me how the book business is doing, assuming local bookstores are a soon-to-be-extinct species.

I soon discover that could not be further from the truth.

When I first start working at Indigo, I have no idea I'll discover such a loyal and impassioned customer base. What really touches me is the enthusiasm.

It's easy to think that modern entertainments like television and social media and podcasts have taken over and killed off books—but far from dampening interest, the explosion of book coverage on platforms like TikTok and Instagram has only helped whet readers' appetites.

It's so inspiring to witness the shared passion over well-loved titles and favorite authors.

The day a new title comes out, I talk to twenty people about how thrilled they are to read this latest book. The same customers come back every time there's a big new release, and their excitement has me eagerly reaching for the books myself. They help me rediscover the enchantment of cracking open a new book and diving headfirst into adventures and love and suspense. Of letting myself marvel at the wonder of fantasy and sigh over heart-melting romance stories.

One of my best customers is a young girl named Maya, a teenager from the nearby high school. She comes to the store alone or with friends, each visit dedicated to looking for new reads. Local students are one of our store's largest demographics. It makes me so happy to see how much the next generation loves reading.

Maya frequently walks over on her lunch break or after school to browse the shelves of her favorite genres, YA and fantasy. The moment she realizes a book she has been wanting is finally available, she squeals with joy.

I eye the stack of books Maya brings up to the cash register today. At least ten volumes. *She must spend all her part-time-job earnings on books,* I think, knowing how often she comes in and how many books she buys.

"I read really fast," Maya says with a laugh as she hands me a rolled-up wad of cash. "And a couple of these are books for my friend too. I told her that she *has* to read these!"

Gloria, who comes in monthly for her Harlequin romance fix, probably ties with Maya for the title of Best Customer.

We have a very strong Harlequin romance following at our location, so much so that we have a call list to announce new arrivals. Gloria's one of several customers on that list.

And we will *certainly* hear about it if we're ever late getting in the titles.

A little while ago, our monthly shipment of Harlequin novels was delivered to the wrong store. We were inundated with calls from irate fans checking in daily until the situation was resolved.

Do not stand in the way of readers and their favorite books!

Erin Duffy

Erin Duffy is the store manager at Barnes & Noble in Tempe, Arizona.

I'm looking for a book called *Fifty Shades of Grey*."

This woman is the third person this week who has asked for that book. It's early 2012.

"We don't carry it," I say.

"Really? Why not?"

"Well, it's mostly an ebook. Print copies are hard to get, and they're mostly only available via what we call print-on-demand. In other words, it's sort of self-published, and our store only carries titles from major publishers."

"That's a shame," the woman says. "All my friends are talking about it."

Another woman comes in a couple of days later and asks my manager for *Fifty Shades of Grey*.

"I'm sorry, we don't carry it," my manager says.

The woman is shocked. My manager starts to explain the whole ebook thing when the woman cuts her off.

"I don't care about any of that," the woman says, her tone bordering on outrage. "This book is going to be *huge*. You need to carry it!"

I do some research and discover that *Fifty Shades of Grey* originally started out as online fan fiction based on the enormously popular Twilight series. The author, E. L. James, rewrote her fanfic into what became *Fifty Shades of Grey*—and it seems to have a growing following online.

This could be something big.

My hunch is correct. Three weeks later, I'm flipping through *Entertainment Weekly* and read an article that says rights to the *Fifty Shades of Grey* trilogy have been picked up for seven figures by Vintage, a prestige imprint at Random House. I show the article to my manager.

"Seems like that lady was right," my manager says.

The print-on-demand book is available for $30. We order copies and stock them on our shelves.

They sell out quickly.

When the book is officially published by Random House, it becomes a monster success. It's hard keeping the book in stock.

I love romance. *Love* it. Romance is one of our store's top-selling categories, and I'm very proud of that because romance is my section. I have an endcap with my name on it recommending my favorite books.

Romance novels still carry a stigma, though. People look at covers with scantily clad men and women embracing and think, *That's junk. There's nothing redeeming about reading romance, it's just sex, sex, sex.*

"There's more to them than just sex," I keep telling doubters. "They're hopeful—and given the world we're living in now, we need hope. And there is absolutely nothing wrong with reading for pleasure. For an escape."

📖

I think back to my early twenties, when I worked at a coffee shop in the morning and at Barnes & Noble in the afternoons and evenings.

One morning, I'm talking about books with a regular customer when she suggests starting a book exchange right here at the coffee shop. I think it's a great idea, so I buy a little bookcase, and the two of us fill it with books.

During a break, I pick a random book off the shelf and take a seat at a nearby table. The book in my hands is *Tempt Me at Twilight* by Lisa Kleypas. The cover features a woman in a wedding dress with a flowing skirt.

A trashy romance novel, clearly.

I've always loved reading—my mother has been reading to me since I was a kid. But this kind of book is what my mother reads, not me. She loves romance novels, yet even she thinks they're trashy.

I start scanning the pages to see what the story is about, and I land on a scene where two characters are in the middle of an actual, physical fight. They're rolling around on the ground, hitting each other, while another character's making jokes that have me laughing out loud.

And I can't stop reading. I don't want to put the book down.

Tempt Me at Twilight becomes the book that starts my official romance journey.

It's funny—when *Fifty Shades* first takes off, people have no problem coming in asking for a copy of what the media calls "mommy porn" and "the Great Idiot American Novel." Customers, I've discovered over the years, are more uncomfortable asking for self-help books.

Still, we keep plenty of copies of *Fifty Shades* behind the front counter for anyone too embarrassed to be seen carrying the book to the register. Some customers call ahead to reserve their copy. As with all phone orders, we put each name on a slip of paper and set a copy aside.

A woman steps up to the front counter and looks around to make sure there's no one within hearing distance. Then she turns to me and says, nervously, "I'm here to pick up a book."

"Sure, what's your last name?"

She gives it to me. I go look for her book.

"Sorry, I can't seem to find it," I apologize.

"The person I spoke to said she'd put it aside."

"What's the name again?"

She repeats her last name and spells it for me.

I still can't find it.

"Let's try this another way," I say. "What's the name of the book?"

The woman looks mortified. Like she would rather die than tell me.

"I can't believe you people! You promised you'd put it aside for me!"

"Is this it?" I ask, and discreetly show her a copy of *Fifty Shades of Grey*.

"*No!*" she nearly screams. "It's called *This Is Why You're Fat*. That's the book I ordered. *This Is Why You're Fat*. I can't believe you didn't put it on hold!"

I find the book. We did, in fact, put it on hold. We'd just misspelled her last name.

Cappy Yarbrough

Carolyn Ann Parham "Cappy" Yarbrough is the publicity assistant at Chronicle Books. She was formerly the children's department manager for Eagle Harbor Book Company on Bainbridge Island, Washington.

I have a very complicated relationship with books.

Growing up, we don't have cable, so every night the whole family piles into my twin brother's room. While my mom knits, my father, the biggest reader I know, reads aloud to the family for hours on end. We like series about wizards—J.K. Rowling's Harry Potter, the Discworld novels by Sir Terry Pratchett, and tales set in J. R. R. Tolkien's Middle-earth. After *The Hobbit*, my dad goes straight into the Lord of the Rings trilogy and finishes reading the final installment to us right as I enter the first grade.

I love the stories that books contain, but learning to read them...it's a struggle. An *intense* struggle.

We live on picturesque Bainbridge Island, a thirty-minute ferry ride from the city of Seattle. I love where I live and I love my school, but neither is equipped to deal with students who have learning difficulties. My mom turns into an absolute warrior advocate for me. She takes me to see all sorts of specialists.

My difficulty, I'm finally told, has a name. Dyslexia. When it comes to reading and writing, my brain has a difficult time deciphering letters and putting them into the correct order, which is why the words always look so confusing to me. It's not until almost the start of fourth grade that, with the help of a tutor, I finally learn to read.

Instead of making me recoil from books, my struggle with dyslexia ignites a passion in me for reading.

My parents take me to Eagle Harbor Book Company. The midsize bookstore is on Main Street, right near the ferry, and gets a lot of foot traffic. I buy a Step into Reading book about Helen Keller. I read it a million times. Same with Mary Pope Osborne's Magic Tree House series. I fall in love with Peggy Parish's Amelia Bedelia books.

It's a beautiful thing. For my parents, reading is like breathing. Our home is covered in books. Mom and Dad are constantly talking about what they're reading. To be able to join in on these conversations makes me feel like I'm truly a part of the family.

In May 2020, I graduate with a master's degree in history from the College of Charleston, in South Carolina. Earning my master's is a huge, personal victory for me, especially because of my dyslexia.

Knowing I'm going to spend the next six months working on PhD applications, I decide to pack up and drive alone across the country to live back at home in Washington with my parents.

The last time I was home, over Christmas break, my father and I stopped in at Eagle Harbor Book Company. As I followed my dad down the aisles, I remembered all the midnight premieres I attended here for the new Harry Potter and Twilight books.

"So, Cappy, read anything good lately?" my dad asked me.

"For pleasure?" I scoffed. What with college and grad school, it had been at least five years since I'd had time to read for fun. "I feel like I can't even connect to books anymore."

"Well, if you could read something for pleasure, what would it be?"

"I don't know," I said. "I guess I really want to read more books by female authors."

"Okay," he said as we wandered down the science fiction section. He stopped at a shelf and plucked out a book.

"Take this," he said, handing me a collection of short stories by Ursula K. Le Guin. She's won all sorts of impressive awards, from a Newbery Honor to the National Book Foundation's Medal for Distinguished Contribution to American Letters.

The book was life-changing. Le Guin quickly becomes my favorite author.

"Okay," my dad says, "the next person you need to read is Octavia Butler."

Butler becomes my second-favorite author.

It's no coincidence, I think, that Le Guin and Butler both lived nearby in the Pacific Northwest. There's something magical here. Something that really sparks creativity and beauty. It's just so special.

"Okay, Dad, now I want to read more nonfiction written by women."

"I have just the person. Joan Didion."

He goes to Eagle Harbor Books and buys me a beautiful copy of Didion's *Slouching Towards Bethlehem*. One night after dinner, my mom's best friend texts me.

"OMG Eagle Harbor Books is hiring. You would be PERFECT."

I get the application that night and bring it into the store the next day. I start work two days later.

To work in a bookstore, you have to know so much—the range of subjects and categories that indicate where on the shelf each book belongs, the content of the inventory.

An older woman tells me her grandchild has come out as nonbinary, and she's really frustrated that so many people are misgendering her grandkid.

"We have this really great graphic novel about they/them pronouns," I say.

I show her the book. She buys ten copies so she can hand them out to everyone.

Another customer comes in, a woman looking for a title I don't recognize. I look it up and see that the book was published about twenty years ago.

"Can you order it for me?" the woman asks.

"I'm afraid I can't, because it's out of print."

"I don't understand," she says. "Everyone is reading it. I saw Bill O'Reilly interview the author on an episode of *The O'Reilly Factor*."

Presumably a rerun, as I know that show has been off the air for some time. Still, I do my best to help the customer find what she's looking for. "What's the book about?"

"It's by a woman who says the CIA brainwashed her."

I dig a little deeper. The book is a self-published memoir that delves into political conspiracy theories. It's not available through regular retail channels, but it's out there online, given the accessibility of self-publishing, the internet, and social media.

"I don't know what I'm going to do. I don't have a computer," the woman says.

I take a deep breath. "I feel an obligation to tell you that I don't believe the information in this book is very sound. But let's come up with a plan. If you really want this book, my suggestion is to go to the library. You can use one of their computers to go online and look for it."

The woman sticks out her hand. "Okay. You've been very helpful. What's your name?"

"Carolyn Ann Parham Yarbrough, but everyone calls me Cappy."

"I really appreciate you taking the time to explain this to me, and for treating me with respect."

I do go the extra mile to treat people with respect. It's not always a two-way street. Some customers get confrontational if we don't have certain books on hand, even if they're not interested in buying them. They just want to see them on the shelf.

I am very levelheaded about my buying choices. I know what my customers want, and what sells well and what doesn't, so I'm not going to apologize for it. And I will help anyone, even though people don't always appreciate the effort and the labor that goes into it.

A good number of customers don't seem to understand that at the end of the day, we're a small, locally owned business. We don't have a warehouse manned by robots. Customers are confused—and sometimes downright angry—that a book they ordered the night before isn't ready to be picked up first thing in the morning.

When January arrives, I'm told I'll be buying books for the kids' department.

The bookstore is a safe space for kids to learn life-related skills, coming on their own after school, counting out change for their purchases, or asking booksellers for a certain title.

Sometimes they're disappointed to learn that a particular book is not in stock.

"I'll have to order it," I say. "It will be here in two days."

It's a hard lesson for some kids, especially when so many material wishes are now granted in an instant. On the flip side, some kids have the patience to wait months for Tui T.

Sutherland's new Wings of Fire book or another big release, and they get so excited they're hyperventilating, crying, or freaking out when the book finally comes in.

A grandmother visits with her grandson.

"He's seven," she says to me. "We've been reading a lot of books. I've been reading aloud to him, and I'm hoping for some recommendations for some new books."

I smile. "We can definitely do that." I look to the boy and say, "Well, my friend, tell me what you like. Do you like fantasy books or do you like books that are more realistic, stories that could happen in real life?"

Without missing a beat, the seven-year-old looks at me and says, "I like realistic fiction with an emotional twist."

His grandmother nods. "Yeah, he does."

"Well, my friends," I say, "the good news is we definitely have that. Let's go find you some." And they leave with four new books.

Patrick Nichol

Patrick Nichol is a navy vet and a bookseller at
Indigo Shawnessy in Calgary, Alberta, Canada.
He was a founding member of the original
Chapters team to launch at that same location
on Halloween in 1998 and has been there
ever since.

Being a bookseller is a lot of fun, but it was a steep learning curve for me.

After leaving the navy, I spend fourteen years as a newspaper reporter. Then in 1998, after moving back to my hometown of Calgary to help my father out after my mother died, I see an ad seeking booksellers for a new location of Chapters—Canada's national bookstore chain—and jump at the chance to join the team.

I'm thrilled to work in a building with hundreds of square

feet of fabulous books. I even like their corporate uniform, a stylish denim shirt with a unique book logo.

I'm hired to handle magazine displays for the newsstand and to act as a store lead, running operations in the absence of management. While I have some limited retail experience from being in the news business, the book trade has all sorts of new moving parts to learn, like how to order books from publishers and merchandising standards. It's a full plate.

In 2001, I load my plate even higher, completing studies at Ryerson University and our Master Bookseller program the same year that rival booksellers Chapters and Indigo are merging. Everything feels a little unsure; we're all wondering where we'll fit in the new organization.

No day that year feels more unstable than September 11. It's a beautiful morning, with a cloudless, brilliant-blue sky as I drive to work. Then suddenly, all the radio stations—even Country 105—are breaking in with stories about an airplane hitting the World Trade Center in New York City.

As a former journalist, I'm riveted.

At that time, Chapters offers internet café access for a fee. For a toonie (a $2 coin), anyone can come in and surf the internet, which is how we're getting the most up-to-date news. Shortly after the second plane hits the WTC, online traffic spikes. All our computer servers crash. It's an exhausting, emotional day, but there's comfort in talking to customers and commiserating about our concerns.

Books have always been ingrained in my life. I especially gravitate to science fiction and to military history, given my own background as a veteran.

One of my fondest interactions is with an elderly gentleman, one of my regular customers. He comes in weekly to buy military history magazines and books. We always chat about various military topics, peppered with my own experiences, and I make a habit of setting aside for him certain books that I know he'll like.

One day, not long after I hear that he's passed away, the man's wife comes into the store and seeks me out.

She tells me that he's gifted me his library. I'm incredibly touched, and I still own that library today.

After twenty-five years in the same location, I know many of my customers quite well. In fact, some were kids when I started, and now they bring their own kids to shop from me.

Over the years, I've also become friends with many authors—one of my favorites is a horror writer named Dana Fredsti, who started out as a stunt performer in the original *Army of Darkness* film. I'm proud to say I regularly hand-sell her novels, and she now even includes me in her acknowledgments.

My love of sci-fi started when I was a young boy, watching *Star Trek* and reading comic books, dreaming of what the future might hold—the realm of possibilities that could happen.

A young comic book fan recently approached me, wearing a T-shirt from the latest Spidey Universe film.

"I loved the movie," he tells me. "Do you guys carry any Spider-Man stories?"

"Oh buddy, you asked the right guy," I say as I lead him over to a compendium of the original Amazing Spider-Man stories created by Stan Lee and Steve Ditko in the 1960s.

I tap the book cover. "Have you heard of Stan Lee, the guy behind most of the Marvel characters in the movies?" The guy nods. "I met him in person—three times!" I say.

He's delighted by both the book and my story.

I enjoy taking part in the annual Calgary Comic & Entertainment Expo, where we occasionally have a vendor's table. When I've got my white beard grown out and I'm heavier, I'm frequently mistaken for fantasy author George R. R. Martin, whose A Song of Ice and Fire series is the basis for HBO's blockbuster *Game of Thrones*. One year during the expo, the expo showrunner actually sends a staffer to ask my boss, "Do you have George R. R. Martin at your table?"

Apparently, after spotting me at our bookselling table, dozens of expo patrons were quizzing the showrunner and his staff about why "George" wasn't on the program.

For years now, I'll raise his author photo up to my face and joke with customers, "Thank you for buying a copy of my book."

Lillian Dabney

*Lillian Dabney is the adult services librarian for
the Seattle Athenaeum, a membership library in
Pike Place Market, in Seattle, Washington.*

Library jobs are very hard to come by. Maybe since adult
librarians never want to retire, because we want to stay in
the book world as long as we can.

In my previous professional life, as a physical therapist
and federal government worker, I always had the feeling of
books pulling me and drawing me in. I became interested in
working at an independent library, where the environment
was a little bit different from that of a public library, so when
an opportunity comes along, I think, *Well, I'll try it.* I've been
very happy here.

The Seattle Athenaeum is a small, intimate library with
about 1,200 or so books, all donations from local estates or

people downsizing. Founder David Brewster, a socially minded person, established this nonprofit member library in 2014 as part of his mission to support the Seattle arts scene.

It wasn't until the 1830s that free public libraries started appearing in America, mostly due to nineteenth-century industrialist Andrew Carnegie, who came along and said, "We need to do something for the working class." But a century earlier, in 1731, when Benjamin Franklin was searching for a way around the high cost of importing books from Europe, he formed a "society of mutual improvement" and established a subscription reading room called the Library Company of Philadelphia.

The idea of access—in exchange for an annual fee—to more books than any one person could afford quickly caught on, and other membership libraries opened in cities like Boston, Charleston, and Philadelphia. Today, there are a dozen or so open for reciprocal membership. Most of them, like the Boston Athenaeum and the New York Society Library, are along the Eastern Seaboard, but there are three west of the Mississippi: two in California and us in Seattle. Before we started in 2014, the last subscription library to open did so over a hundred years earlier, in 1899.

Our first location is near the Seattle Public Library–Central Library. There isn't a lot of foot traffic over on Fourth Avenue, so when the athenaeum's lease ends, we move to Pike Place Market. It's such a unique location.

Some athenaeums have a special focus. For instance, the Athenaeum Music & Arts Library in San Diego County is dedicated, as its name suggests, to the arts.

We have a strong collection of books about the Pacific Northwest. People in Seattle love Seattle, and they love anything about Seattle. A lot of our circulation is books about the Pacific Northwest or by authors who have written about the Pacific Northwest, like Jess Walter, Garth Stein, Neal Stephenson, and Maria Semple. I'd love for us to focus on translated literature, because Seattle has become a hub for international translators. I always point to Jay Rubin, a local who's translated many books by bestselling and award-winning Japanese author Haruki Murakami. It's one of my missions as a librarian, bringing literature in translation to people, showing them voices from other places. There are so many stories out there that people are missing when they're not translated.

An organization called Northwest Translators & Interpreters Society (NOTIS) meets at our library. They're lovely. Every time I'm around them, I want to join their community and be in their clique. I'm not a translator, but that doesn't stop me from thinking, *They're amazing. They're just amazing.*

Translations have been growing in recognition. For example, since 2015 the International Booker Prize in the UK has been awarded annually for fiction translated into English. And the translator's name has begun to appear on the front cover alongside the author's. They've started to be appreciated for their unique skill, which has its own basis in the craft of writing.

I love authors. I think they are magical. People read books and say, *Oh, this is really good.* But I don't think they realize how much work goes into writing a book. So much care and thought goes into every book. These authors are forward-thinking, they're exploring humanity. They're doing so many things that we should be doing, and they're helping us do it by writing these incredible books.

My recharge button is reading. But, hey, there are so many books to read. I have no hesitation about not finishing a book. I could be three-fourths of the way through and if I'm feeling, *This is not doing it,* I'll close it and go on to another book. And I feel confident enough as a reader that I can tell within the first fifty pages, sometimes even less, whether a book is going to engage me or not. So no, I don't have to finish a book, because authors keep writing and publishers keep publishing new books.

Another mission of mine is to promote critical thinking. In my book discussion groups, I use a technique that was developed by the Great Books Foundation in Chicago. It's called Shared Inquiry. I don't go in asking, "Well, what did you think about the book?" I have specific questions to get people to look deeper. Readers in my groups end up not only understanding the book—they end up understanding other people, other cultures. They end up understanding themselves.

I'm an active reader. I read one book at a time. If I'm reading it in preparation for one of my in-house book discussion groups, or if I'm reading it to interview the author, I take notes and make a list of personalized questions. I give my full attention to that one book. I get totally immersed. Even when we have a busy schedule of events and I feel overwhelmed, I keep reminding myself that this is what I love to do.

I love to read. I love authors. I love to talk about their books. I could talk about books forever.

Taylor Rose Berry

Taylor Rose Berry is the owner and operator of
Berry & Co. in Sag Harbor Village, New York.

I had no intention of going into the book business.

Babylon Village on Long Island, where I grew up, is, as the locals say, a drinking village with a fishing problem. I start working at age thirteen and spend my summers in nearby Sag Harbor, busing tables and waitressing. I help open a few great restaurants and quickly become successful in the hospitality industry, but by age twenty-five, I'm already feeling burned out.

"Why don't you work at the bookstore?" my husband says. "You love books."

It's true. I've always been a prolific reader. Even in pictures of me as a toddler, I'm always carrying a book. Before I dropped out of college, I signed up for every available class in post-modern literature, creative writing, and journalism.

Books have always been my safe haven. Growing up as the only child of divorced parents, reading was—and still is—an escape. A sanctuary and a safe place.

I end up working at BookHampton in nearby East Hampton. I fall in love with the job. It's an aha moment, realizing that I've always loved giving other people book recommendations. I've always been a bookseller. Seeing customers who love books the same way I do is fantastic, an occupational joy, even though there's not a lot of money in this work.

Very quickly, I rise through the ranks. Three years later, I open my own store in Sag Harbor. I negotiate a five-year lease on a very expensive building on Main Street.

It's 2014. I'm determined to open my new bookstore, which I name Harbor Books, on Black Friday.

We have twenty-two days to make it happen.

Call me crazy, ballsy—or just really lucky. But we push through with that insane schedule, even pulling an all-nighter to get everything ready for the grand opening.

The next morning, on Black Friday, people are knocking down our door. The owner of the American Hotel across the street sends over four cases of champagne to celebrate.

It's great. Magical. So many writers and artists come by to wish us well. Sag Harbor is a very literary community—it's always fascinating to see how many authors and agents either live in the area or come by to visit—but when I open in 2014, there's only one other bookstore in town. Though it sells some new titles, it's mostly a used-book shop. Which makes my job coming in as a new indie bookseller even easier.

The space looks fantastic, and I'm so proud of the hard work I put into curating the books on the shelves. In addition to recent bestsellers and personal favorites (I'm always drawn to true crime), I've made sure to stock classic books of local interest.

James Fenimore Cooper was a full-time whaler and part-time writer when he moved to Sag Harbor in 1818 before writing *The Last of the Mohicans*. John Steinbeck arrived in 1955 with his dog, the standard poodle made famous by *Travels with Charley*. Customers can browse works of the "Sagg Main Set"—George Plimpton, Kurt Vonnegut, Truman Capote, and other writers who over the years lived in nearby Sagaponack—and contemporary Hamptons fiction like Colson Whitehead's *Sag Harbor*.

I've thought of everything that could possibly happen and everything anyone can possibly need.

Two hours into the grand opening, a customer walks in and asks for a copy of *The Great Gatsby*.

Not only is *The Great Gatsby* a perennial classic, it is *the* quintessential story of Long Island's Gold Coast during the Jazz Age.

I forgot to order it. How could I have let that happen?

I call it the Gatsby moment.

That weekend is trial by fire. I learn a lot of valuable and important lessons.

Outsiders tend to assume that Sag Harbor is a super-liberal community. The truth is, people here are as diverse as their reading tastes. Books by Bill O'Reilly are huge sellers at the store. So is Paulo Coelho's *The Alchemist*—I sell two copies a day, no matter what. The way women read *Fifty Shades of Grey,* you'd think the author was starting a cult. There are certain books I always have on the shelves, childhood favorites of mine like *Gone with the Wind* or *I Capture the Castle.* I love to recommend J. R. Moehringer's *The Tender Bar,* and I keep two dozen copies on hand. But mainly I prefer to let the customers dictate. I think it's foolish not to listen to your audience.

From the beginning, I decide not to select books based solely on my own philosophical, sociological, and political beliefs. There are independent bookstores that editorialize their collections—that's the joy of being an independent bookseller, you can do whatever you want—but it's important to me that customers can walk into the store and find a little bit of everything, so to speak.

I work hard to ensure a balance, for instance carrying both Elie Wiesel's Holocaust memoir *Night* and Hitler's *Mein Kampf.* I want all points of view to be represented, the extremes and everything in between. Not everyone agrees. People have strong feelings about my choices.

"When someone buys *Mein Kampf,* who do you report it to?" a person might ask.

"I don't report it to anyone." Who would I report to? Any book has the potential to be dangerous, no matter the subject. The flip side is that all politics aside, I think banning books is wildly dangerous. Books are the foundation of our society.

I don't protest much, but when people start banning books, I'll be standing on the picket lines.

I attend the wedding of a bestselling author and her longtime boyfriend. They get married on a vintage yacht in Sag Harbor. The event is being covered by *Vogue*.

When the boat docks, everyone drunkenly walks to my bookstore, where the bride is going to do a toast. I stand in the middle of the store, barefoot in a gown, and pour champagne for everyone.

The guest list is full of *New York Times* bestselling authors. Given my location in the Hamptons, authors come into my store all the time, and I get to swoon in their presence. Even though it happens often, it's still really special. I think it can be hard for introverted writers to be gawked at, but selling their books is so much easier when we meet them and love them.

At one point near midnight, I look around and realize that all of these brilliant and amazing writers dressed in tuxedos and beautiful dresses are standing together in my store, all holding each other's books and bickering good-naturedly, laughing and drinking and signing books for one another.

I savor the remarkable moment.

Sag Harbor, I've realized, isn't a village with a bookstore. It's a village that *is* a bookstore.

I love putting books in everybody's hands, even the people who aren't necessarily looking for them. There's nothing better than finding the right book for the right person and seeing how it lights them up and changes them. I've always said that the relationship with your bookseller is somewhere in between a bartender, a priest, a therapist.

It's about trust.

I love when people tell me they're "difficult readers" and insist that I'll never be able to find a book that they'll like, and then all of a sudden they're coming back to me saying, "That was the best book I ever read. What am I going to read next?"

When my five-year lease is up, I decide to switch gears a bit. I shutter Harbor Books and open Berry & Co. on an adjacent street. With Berry & Co., I'm focusing on more bespoke book sales that aren't being fulfilled by traditional bookselling. I can make bookselling a more personal experience without being explicitly tied to a brick-and-mortar store. Now I can rove anywhere I want and continue doing what I love—matching people with books.

Catrina Haynes

Catrina Haynes is a district manager for Books-A-Million in Tampa, Florida.

I'm looking for a book for my daughter," a woman says.

She's perusing our BookTok table—we've got a full-sized feature table dedicated to the popular social media recommendations, plus sixteen feet of BookTok-endorsed titles separated by category: romance, spicy romance, sci-fi, fantasy, young adult.

"Great, how old is she?" I ask, eyeing the young adult section.

"Well, she's ten, but she's reading at a tenth-grade level," the mother says proudly.

Hmm, I think. *It's wonderful that she's reading at that level...but do you really want your ten-year-old kid reading the same book as a sixteen-year-old?*

It's a tricky position.

When I was a preteen, my mom was reading V. C. Andrews's *Flowers in the Attic*. It was a bestseller and had a lot of buzz—there's an incestuous relationship in it, not graphic or anything, but very salacious—and I wanted to read it *so* badly.

I've always been an avid reader; my parents told me stories about how, long before I could actually read, I'd memorize the books they read to me, then would sit and "read" the books to myself. My dad was in the air force and we moved around a lot, so at many times in my childhood I considered books my best friends. I may have been in an unfamiliar place, but I could always go back and read that Judy Blume book or that Beverly Cleary book again and find my friends there.

Anyway, my mom had *Flowers in the Attic* and I wanted to read it, but she wouldn't let me.

"No, you can't read that. You're not old enough to read it."

Guess who read *Flowers in the Attic* as soon as her mom left for work? This girl. I went on to devour everything that V. C. Andrews ever wrote. In fact, I still have my mom's original set of the first four Flowers in the Attic paperbacks. And I've reread them many times over in my adult life as well.

So kids are always going to have that urge to sneak books that aren't age-appropriate.

Do I think that there's such a thing as age-appropriate content? Absolutely. I can't decide for a parent what their child reads, but I can make recommendations. Then it's up to the parent to decide what they want to allow for their own child.

But when someone else says, "Your kid can't read that," well, that doesn't sit right with me.

I believe we should be equal-opportunity booksellers. If we start saying, "Oh, we're not selling that author's book in the store," then we're going down the wrong path. As long as it's in print, we can sell anybody's book, get any book that a customer wants.

I've been with Books-A-Million for fifteen years. Before that, I worked in real estate for thirteen years, but when the market starts to crash in 2007, I decide it's time to make a switch. *If I'm going to change careers,* I tell myself, *then I want to make sure it's something that I like.*

I'm a reader and a crafter, so I apply at craft stores and bookstores.

Books-A-Million intrigues me the most, because the real estate office I'm leaving was a family-run business, and at heart, regardless of how many stores we have, Books-A-Million is also still a family business.

I'm hired as a manager in training, into what at that time was the highest-volume store in our company. I quickly learn that the family feeling throughout the organization is genuine—the family within a store, the family within a district, the family within a region—and we're small enough that, unlike in a larger corporation, I know pretty much everybody. I know them on a more personal level, I know their kids' names, I know if they have a dog. They're not strangers I'm only reaching out to because I need something, or they need something from me.

Now as a district manager, I'm typically on the road four days a week, Tuesday through Friday, with Mondays in the home office. Let's be honest, sometimes it's not the most fun to get on a plane at five a.m. or drive four hours to Tallahassee. There are some days where I'm like, "Ugh."

But once I get to the stores, I'm with my people and that's where I want to be. Their excitement for the job gets *me* excited. Our buyers, our merchants, are some of the most amazing people I've ever met. They are so in tune with the trends. They give us the information that we need, they provide us with the product, and then we're able to sell it. You think you're just showing up for work and customers will just go to the shelves and buy the books, but that's not the case.

Each store is a little bit different in what they're able to do. One of my stores has a service-dog program: once a month, the dogs—who normally visit nursing homes and children's hospitals—come in on a Saturday and have story time with the kids. The kids sit down and read while they're petting these dogs. It's very comforting for the kids. They love it. Parents love it.

I've really learned how intimate a book purchase can be. When somebody's getting excited about something, I'm like, "Oh, show me," or if they want to talk about a book, then I want to talk about that book with them. And there's the joy we both feel when we find the exact title they came in looking for.

They can't wait to come back and talk about their next book.

Karen Roy

*Karen Roy has been a medical research librarian
and a children's librarian. She has worked around
the country and now lives in New York City.*

In forty-four years as a librarian, I've met a lot of parents
whose kids don't like reading. When these parents ask me
to recommend books, I suggest the perennial favorites: Beverly Cleary, Gary Paulsen, the Newbery Award winners, the
Caldecott Medal winners, et cetera. I always prefer to interest
kids in prolific authors, because if kids like one of an author's
books, then they're typically going to want to read them all.

But then I get more inquisitive.

Do you read to them? I ask the parents. *Do they see you
reading to yourself? Do you subscribe to a newspaper or magazine? Do you take them to the local library?*

I give all the credit to my wonderful mother for leading me

to my library career. She read to me and my six siblings constantly, took us to the library constantly. She besotted all of us with words—of her seven children, two become teachers, three become journalists, one a poet, and me, a librarian.

When I'm in high school, I work in a public library, and then I go to college right down the road. I work in two successive schools of nursing libraries, which lands me my first job out of college at Tulane's medical library in New Orleans.

In those days, borrowers sign out their books, so part of my job at the checkout desk is to quickly memorize the student or doctor's name as scripted on their white lab coats. After they leave, I print their names on the line below their indecipherable scrawls.

In the 1980s, I work at Harvard's Countway Library in Boston. There, the doctors, students, and researchers affiliated with Harvard Medical School, Harvard School of Public Health, and Harvard School of Dental Medicine are required to make appointments with librarians. They outline the focus of their investigations, and we librarians laboriously search through printed periodical indices.

Later, I switch to being a children's school librarian in New York and in Florida. Oh, it is so much fun. I love working with kids, nursery school age up through teens. "Let me know what you're working on in class, and I'll find books to support you," I tell the teachers. I especially enjoy story time with the younger students. They can produce startlingly beautiful drawings of a just-heard story or listen to tapes of whales communicating and then reproduce the squawks and clicks.

Middle school students can cut up our local newspaper to answer a job ad, or comment on current events or sports. It's okay to talk in library class with your tablemates. I want to give them a voice.

I marvel at the ingenuity of many students' research topics. Children have such a wonderful ability to devise fresh extensions to new information. I learn so much from their free-wheeling imagination and so appreciate sponsoring the awe of discovery and helping spark the flame of creativity.

I'm especially drawn to the new kids, who, when they're finding their way in a new school, often come to the library instead of going to lunch with their classmates. I try to draw them out.

"Hey, what are you reading? Have you tried this?" I ask. They're just looking for a listening ear, a warm welcome. If I can, I'll add a nudge—"Oh, Joe Schwartz really likes that topic. You might ask him about it"—trying to introduce to them the idea of, Hey, branch out. See what happens.

I try hard to follow my own advice when I also become the computer teacher. I scramble to learn the intricacies of computers since I'm now the guide on the side, no longer the sage on the stage. No surprise, the kids learn more quickly than I do; I often ask students to lead the computer classes, and I learn right along with them. It's encouraging to know that if we've made a mistake, we can all just hit the little backward arrow in the top left corner or try edit, undo.

"Who dares to teach must never cease to learn" is a magnificent quotation from the librarian John Cotton Dana in

1912. Dana, who's referred to as the father of the modern library, converted libraries from the sanctuaries of the wealthy, dues-paying, lettered clientele to bustling community centers.

I have book club this afternoon at my local library. We just finished *The Four Winds* by Kristin Hannah, a novel set during the Great Depression. Next, we're reading *The Personal Librarian* by Marie Benedict and Victoria Christopher Murray, historical fiction set in Gilded Age New York about J. P. Morgan's personal librarian, Belle da Costa Greene.

When it's my turn to choose, I'll pick a nonfiction book about science or biography or history. I don't read much fiction. I get too impatient. I want the facts.

Anne Holman

Anne Holman is a co-owner of the King's English Bookshop in Salt Lake City, Utah.

Our bookstore, a blue cottage with a gray roof and peaked dormers, is counting down to midnight. It's only a few hours until the fourth Harry Potter book will be released.

The tiny shopping block has been transformed into one of the beloved locations from the series, Diagon Alley: a hidden cobblestoned area of London where young students bound for Hogwarts School of Witchcraft and Wizardry visit to purchase their wands, brooms, books, and other magical items.

We've had midnight release parties for other new books—the latest novels in the Twilight series by Stephenie Meyer and Christopher Paolini's Inheritance Cycle, featuring the adventures of a boy and his dragon. At those events, adults accompanied their children, happy to encourage a love of reading.

But at Harry Potter parties, there are plenty of adults who are here for themselves. They're just as excited as the youngsters to get their hands on the newest Harry Potter.

I've never seen a line this long. It stretches around the block, the kind of line you'd usually see for the most popular ride at Disney. Only these people are waiting in line to purchase a *book*.

Children and adults of all ages and ethnicities walk underneath the string lights decorating the trees. The surrounding stores have been given names straight out of the Harry Potter books, with some of the owners joining in on the fun too. Everyone is in a festive mood, dressed as their favorite characters as they wait for midnight, the time when the newest Harry Potter will officially go on sale.

The clock strikes twelve.

As we start handing out copies, my gaze keeps flitting to a little girl who is probably in the first or second grade. She's dressed like Harry Potter, complete with the cape, glasses, and the lightning scar on her forehead. She's beaming with excitement.

When she gets to the front of the line, I hand her a book. She opens it, moves it close to her face, and inhales deeply, as though I've given her a bouquet of rare, exotic flowers.

"Doesn't it smell great?" she asks.

"Yes, honey, it does," I reply, thinking, *You've got such a great life ahead of you.*

We buy the corner gas station, convert it into our store's children's room, and connect it to our building.

It's a good size, but the children's room still looks like an old gas station. We hear that James Patterson is giving out grants to help independent bookstores. We write a proposal about how we'd like to redo our children's room.

Our proposal is accepted.

With the grant money, we remove the dropped ceiling and purchase new windows. There's an ugly-looking iron pole in the room, but we can't remove it because it supports our furnace. Instead, we decide to turn the pole into an aspen tree, the state tree of Utah, and build a magnificent tree house around it.

We carve James Patterson's initials, along with ours, into the tree: *JP + TKE*.

Our new children's room has been transformed into a beautiful, amazing space. Kids come inside and play under the tree house, surrounded by books, with cozy places where they can sit and read.

I'm working with Margaret, who runs the children's area, when a pair of older male customers approach us. One wears a ski hat. The other has a goatee and long, curly white-and-gray hair that spills across his shoulders.

"Good morning," the one with the goatee says with a bright smile. He has a British accent and wears a stylish silk scarf. "We're both looking for books for our grandchildren, and I was wondering if you could give us some recommendations."

"How old are your grandkids?"

The two give us their grandchildren's ages. As Margaret

and I show them various books, we ask them where they're from, what they're doing in Salt Lake City—polite conversation. People are hovering nearby, watching.

Why are they staring at us?

The two men bring a stack of books to the front counter. As we ring them up, they keep thanking us for our help. By now, nearly everyone in the store is watching our exchange, listening as the two men wish us a pleasant day and a wonderful weekend.

An awkward silence fills the store after they leave.

One of my customers, a woman named Sarah who is around my age, comes up to me and says, "Anne, do you know who that was?"

"Which one?" I ask.

"The man with the scarf and the curly hair."

I shake my head and turn to Margaret. She doesn't have an answer either.

"That man," Sarah says, "was Robert Plant."

My jaw drops. *"From Led Zeppelin?"*

Sarah nods. "That's the one."

I had no idea. I thought he was just a lovely older man looking for books for his grandchildren.

Amy Cheney

Amy Cheney runs the Juvenile Justice Literacy
Project in the San Francisco Bay area of
California. She received the I Love My Librarian
Award from the American Library Association,
the Carnegie Corporation, and the New York
Public Library, and a National Arts and
Humanities Youth Program Award from the White
House.

About ten or fifteen of my activist friends are arrested for protesting nuclear power. They're sent to the Santa Rita Jail, which is a huge jail in the San Francisco Bay Area.

After a couple of days, they're released. They come talk to me.

"I thought about you when I was in jail," they say. "Amy, I was going crazy in there. There wasn't a single book to read! I can't imagine what happens to people who are held there for long periods of time."

I've been working as a library page, basically entry-level, so I research the situation at the jail. Jails are temporary facilities. Someone could be held there for a single day or for five years, but it's still considered short-term. So while a prison, which is more long-term, *might* have a library and other reading programs, jails may have few if any ways to access books.

One major obstacle is that people can't send books to jails or prisons directly. I find one library that services jails and prisons in Alameda County. From them, I learn about the most requested types of books and materials. I organize book drives all over the Bay Area; I'm able to acquire a lot of sought-after books.

A year later, the library employs me to provide service to people in jails and prisons in Alameda County.

I've devoured books as far back as I can remember. Even as a kid, I read a lot of adult books, like John Steinbeck's *East of Eden,* or Dostoyevsky's *Crime and Punishment.* I read a lot about the Holocaust. I have nightmares, and these stories fill me with rage about the appalling crimes against humanity.

I carry that fiery ball of emotions with me throughout my teenage years.

It isn't until I attend a reading in a church basement, where

I hear Maya Angelou read her work aloud, that something fundamentally changes in me. Hearing Maya Angelou speak is life-changing. Despite my teenage resistance to her words, the hard, closed fist living inside my chest begins to open, and I have a realization that my spirit is separate from my rage.

The hardest part of my new job is providing service to the women who are incarcerated. The men are mostly educated about what they want to read: Black history, Westerns, and mysteries. The women seem to only want the perfume samples that come in fashion magazines like *Vogue*. Their low level of literacy keeps me up at night. I want to find a way to connect with them. Support them. I want to find a way to be of service.

I read a book called *Mama* by Terry McMillan. It's her first novel, a story about a fierce, strong, and funny Black woman who throws her drunk husband out of the house and sets about raising her five children on her own. The book takes the world by storm. It crosses over to white readers, showing publishers that there's a wide audience hungry for a great story.

I wonder if McMillan would be willing to speak to the women.

I find her contact information, and somehow she takes my call. I introduce myself and ask her if she'll come out to speak at the jail.

"Yes," she says.

McMillan's visit literally changes everything for these women—and also for me. I can now be of service. Now when I come to work, the women want to engage me in conversation. What am I reading? What books can I recommend? Do I know any other famous authors? What does Terry McMillan read and who are her friends?

The change is so dramatic, I still get goose bumps thinking about it. I start to bring more authors into the jails to speak to both the women and the men. The events are successful, which leads me and my colleagues to consider a new opportunity.

What if we bring these same opportunities to kids? It could be a huge life-changer for some of them.

When I worked with adults enrolled in library literacy programs, I asked them why they felt they had challenges with reading. Every single one of them went into a full-blown trauma response about a negative experience they had with books and reading in school. Their stories all share a common emotion: shame.

And for no good reason.

I'm of the opinion that all people are literate, as all people can communicate and create meaning from words and symbols. They do know *how* to read—the same way they know how stop signs work. They know aspects of reading, like how to turn the pages of a book, but those skills haven't been valued or validated.

Building literacy doesn't even have to start with actual reading. I've seen little kids who insist on carrying around a Harry Potter book or a Paul Auster novel. Maybe they just like the colors on the cover. And that's okay. The important part is that they are identifying as someone who totes around a big book.

It doesn't matter whether or not that child can truly read it. That child is loving that book. We can still celebrate it.

It's all a part of literacy development.

There's something incredibly special about the library and the culture that we create at the juvenile hall.

Tamika comes into my office.

"I don't like to read, and I don't know what to do." She stares at the floor, ashamed.

"Well, what kind of stories do you like?"

"I kind of like...So there was this book that I kind of liked, but I don't remember the title. But I remember it was by Lois Duncan."

"It sounds like you like mysteries, then," I say. Lois Duncan, a master of teen suspense, wrote over a dozen popular YA books like *Don't Look Behind You* and *I Know What You Did Last Summer.*

I set her up with new Lois Duncan mysteries. The books get her animated. Tamika is one of many kids who risk getting in trouble by shouting to me when she's in line and supposed to be silent.

"I'm on page thirty-three!" she yells proudly.

Kai Burner

Kai Burner is the assistant manager, children's buyer, and gifts buyer at the Bookworm of Edwards in Edwards, Colorado.

A fiftysomething man wanders into the Bookworm of Edwards.

He walks up to me. "Hey, I was driving past, saw you here," he says. "Do you want me to sign some books?"

I'm perplexed. *Why would this guy want to sign books?* He sees my confusion and gestures toward a stack of *The Lincoln Highway* and *A Gentleman in Moscow*. "Oh, I'm the author. I'm Amor Towles."

Oh, man. "Oh yeah, sure. Of course!" I say, scrambling to find every single copy of his books that we have in stock. Then he sits in the café for half an hour, sipping a coffee and signing books.

It's a fun little celebrity moment.

Our robust events program gets a lot of authors in the store—both our fantastic local authors and *New York Times* bestselling writers who may stop by when they're in our area, which is about twenty miles outside of Vail. There's a lot of mutual appreciation and respect between booksellers and writers. Authors understand how much power indie booksellers have in the industry and really value our time and opinions. But it's also supercool when they go out of their way to do something nice like just swing by.

I've been working at the Bookworm for six years now, and I absolutely love it.

I went to college in Wyoming, where I majored in psychology—with a minor in religious studies, emphasis on Eastern religions—but after getting my undergrad degree, I'm not so sure I really want to pursue a master's program in psychology or to be a therapist.

I want some time and space to figure things out, so I move back home to Colorado, to live with my parents. I figure I'll give myself a year to decide what I want to do for a career.

In the meantime, though, I need to get a job.

I'm thrilled to spot a job listing at my beloved local bookstore, the Bookworm of Edwards, for a management position. *Working at the bookstore would be so cool,* I think to myself. *I love that place.*

Back when I was little, the Bookworm was a tiny 600-square-foot space that felt like someone's home library. I have many fond childhood memories of sitting on a wooden chair in the corner of the store—one of those chairs that flips over into a stepladder, which I remember thinking was the coolest thing I had ever seen in my entire life—browsing through picture books while my parents shopped.

Even though I don't have the experience, I apply for the manager job anyway.

The owner lets me down gently. "You don't have the qualifications for this position," she tells me, "but I'll keep your application in case any entry-level positions open up."

A bummer, but I understand. About a month later, she emails to say, "We have a frontline bookselling position open. Why don't you come in for an interview?"

I do and am hired that same day.

The area around Vail gets a lot of stereotypical ski town tourist traffic, but Edwards is just far enough away to have a small, local feel. The Bookworm has always had a cozy vibe, even though it's grown enormously since I was a kid, over six times the original size. It's almost 4,000 square feet now and has a café.

The next-closest bookstore is fifty miles away, so we're in a unique position to help serve the community. We do a lot of service. We work with probably a dozen different organizations, like local nonprofits and schools. One of our coolest programs is called Adopt-a-Reader, where customers can anonymously buy books for kids in the valley who don't have access to books in their homes. Every month, a community member will buy a book for a particular child so he or she can build their own personal home library. There are almost two hundred kids in the program right now. We have little bookplates that we put in with the kids' names, so they know the books are theirs and they can keep them.

It's a great opportunity to give kids more ownership of their own literacy, and—even though it's completely anonymous and they'll never meet these kids or see the results firsthand—customers who donate money every month are really invested. Just knowing that they're having that impact is so special.

It's the same for me. Knowing I'm playing a part in making a tangible difference in the lives of these kids—it's an amazing feeling.

We've got a truly supportive community here. They really came together for us during the pandemic in a way that still makes me a little emotional to think about. It was such an uncertain time, especially for a business like an independent bookstore that makes such a small profit every year to begin with. No one is in the book industry to make money.

I come from a family of huge readers. Lawyers, teachers, professors, and journalists. Literacy was super important in our house, and my parents read to me and my older sister all the time. When I turned eight or ten, my father read us one of his favorite trilogies, J. R. R. Tolkien's Lord of the Rings, out loud from start to finish. It rocked my world. Everything changed; that's when I discovered it was possible to fall in love with a book.

Then, a few years later, I stumbled upon a novel from the 1960s called *The Outsiders* by S. E. Hinton. For the entire day, I sat curled up in our living room chair, losing track of time as I read about the whirlwind experiences of Johnny and Ponyboy. I couldn't stop reading, couldn't put the book down.

The Outsiders really cemented my feeling about how incredibly vital books are to my life.

As soon as I was hired at the Bookworm, I made sure to order the book and keep it in stock. I recommend it all the time. I recommend it for book club readers. I recommend it for students who need to find a "classic" novel for English class. I recommend it for kids going through a tough time.

I went through a tough time myself recently. Spending a lot of solo time during the pandemic led me to recognize that I'm trans. It was a scary realization, and I felt adrift.

Then I picked up a copy of *Cemetery Boys* by Aiden Thomas. It's a YA book about a young trans boy trying to find his way in the world, and it had been sitting in my to-be-read pile for months.

I like to say I found the book, but the reality is that the book found me.

Seeing myself through the eyes of the character, a young trans boy who is trying to prove himself to his family and to the world, helped me with my own struggles. It helped me gain perspective on my life. My journey.

The power of seeing yourself represented through someone else's words—that's the power of books.

Books are deeply personal. They're so varied and vast. They

have the power to distract us from our problems and to change our minds, to change our lives. To make us feel less alone.

The act of physically handing someone a book while looking that person in the eye creates an intimate and powerful connection. You're forming a personal bond through the transaction.

"This is what you're looking for," I tell them. "I would bet my life on it. This is what you're going to love."

And then they come back and say, "Okay, what else you got?"

Continuing that conversation about books and authors is one of a bookseller's greatest joys.

PART FIVE

Just one more chapter, please, just
one more chapter.

Emily Schall

Emily Schall is an adult services librarian in the Culture and AV division of the Akron–Summit County Public Library in Akron, Ohio.

O h, you're a librarian. You sit behind a desk all day."

I do sit at a desk sometimes—when people come to the Akron–Summit County Public Library looking for movies and fiction books in the Culture and AV division, I'm one of the librarians who greets patrons—but people don't understand that desk work is only one part of the job.

People underestimate librarians.

We put a lot of work into everything we do, from programming to collection development in our own individual sections. We pull the holds. We make displays. We oversee the hot spots and the laptops. Becoming a public or academic librarian requires getting a master's degree in library science.

Desk time is prime learning time, talking to people about books, seeing what they enjoy, assisting them with whatever they need.

We research. When someone says, "Oh, I like mysteries," I research the subgenres—like cozy mysteries, capers, crime, police procedurals, noir, private detective, and traditional murder mysteries. I use what I've learned to make suggestions to readers.

When they say, "Hey, I really liked that book you told me about," that really makes me smile. That's a happy thing for me.

We have a Library of Things here in my department. I maintain hot spots that people can check out, essentially taking their internet home. We have many computers, which get a ton of usage by the public. I think it'd be really cool if the library could go a little bit more techy for the patrons. I am all for keeping physical books and ebooks—*and* also for moving deeper into the technological world. I think that's the right route, that's the direction the library needs to move in.

Shelving books brings diversity into my own reading. There are so many different genres of books, from literary fiction to romance, from biographies to thrillers. I know it's a little weird, but I can easily go from reading a romance straight into a thriller. I really enjoy finding diverse books.

Strange as it may seem, early on in my life, books were not my thing. That changed in elementary school, when we started taking computerized tests. Points were awarded for answering questions on the books we read as schoolwork—what they were, how they came about. I'm a very competitive person. I wanted to be the head student. I started reading more and more, and that's when my love of books started.

In middle school, I became a library assistant. And then I started two part-time jobs during my junior year of high school: one at the bookstore at the University of Akron and another at my local library. I've worked in libraries ever since.

I feel very lucky to have been basically working in the same place since I was seventeen. I feel like I've picked the correct career for myself.

It hasn't all been peaches and cream—but I would say a lot of it *has* been peaches and cream.

The Akron library is one of the bigger systems in Northeast Ohio, with a main library and eighteen different branches. Before coming here to the main library, I was a teen librarian at the Cuyahoga Falls Library, another library close to the Akron system, so teen books hold a special place in my heart—like *Eleanor & Park,* author Rainbow Rowell's first novel for young adults. Rainbow Rowell is near and dear to me. She's been one of my favorite authors since I was in high school, and I've seen her speak multiple times. I saw her when I went to BookFest in New York.

In my first seven months working here at the main hub, I start a book club called YA for Not So YA. Membership is growing every month, slow but steady. People have a month to read the book we choose, at their own pace. The slower readers can take their time, and the people who read faster can take a couple of days before the book club meeting. Our next book club pick is the *Stranger Things Holiday Specials* graphic novel, based on the *Stranger Things* television series.

Getting to know library regulars is something that I truly do enjoy. Since I'm new, I'm still learning our regulars here. The Haven of Rest Ministries for the homeless is a block or two from the library. Many program participants visit the library daily and spend hours enjoying the amenities, such as air conditioning, shelter, and internet. The people are so nice. They're absolutely wonderful. One gentleman fist-bumps us every single day. They're just wonderful patrons.

During our Akron Book Fest, my cohorts here at the library and I help get books donated and have local authors come do book talks. And we have school visits with the preschools and elementary schools, which helps get the kids interested in coming to the library with their story time. When I was the teen librarian, and also when I worked at the Portage Lakes Branch Library, I used to help out by going to schools and summer programs, which I think truly, truly helps with developing literacy and making the library seem fun and cool to the younger generations, having them get into reading and making the idea of it something to be excited about.

We also have our summer reading program, where you can win prizes for reading. That sort of thing helps keep kids reading—it definitely worked on me.

Pamela Blair

Pamela Blair and her husband are the owners and founders of EyeSeeMe African American Children's Bookstore in St. Louis, Missouri.

My son is in trouble.

Again.

Ezra, my youngest child, is in kindergarten. Nearly every day, I get a note from his teacher about his behavior. Today, he turned on all the faucets in the boys' bathroom and flooded the floor.

He's not a bad kid. The school knows he's bright, and they've placed him in a gifted program. But even though he's reading and doing math at a third-grade level, he's bored and frustrated and continually getting into trouble.

I decide to pull him out of kindergarten. Temporarily.

"I'm going to teach you at home for a couple of weeks," I tell him.

But what, exactly, am I going to teach?

I'm not *in* education, but I'm a stickler *for* education. I want a traditional classroom setting.

Books have always been a big part of our household. The only television is in the master bedroom, and it's not watched often. As a family, we all play games and read together. My husband, Jeffrey, read encyclopedias for fun as a child. I grew up in Guyana, the only English-speaking country in South America, and loved reading books like *The Little Red Hen* and *The Three Little Pigs* before graduating to the Hardy Boys and Nancy Drew.

I know Ezra is supersmart. All my children are—my oldest son started college at age fifteen, and my twin daughters, who are a year older than Ezra, both learned to read by age three. When the school suggests that one of my twins ought to be in special ed, the girls instead join Ezra in homeschooling.

I research existing homeschool curriculums. I connect with other homeschoolers and learn that every parent has a different approach and methodology. I choose a focus: history, a subject I hated in school.

I was twelve when my family immigrated to the United States, to New Jersey. We lived in a predominately Black community, but American culture is vastly different, and it was uncomfortable dealing with all kinds of topics I never had to consider when I was growing up in Guyana. For the first time in my life, I learned to be very much aware of my "Blackness," what it meant to be a Black girl.

My homeschool lesson planning centers on the Black experience. I want my children to know more about their history, and their culture, and where they came from. I want to provide them with a deeper, richer understanding of Black culture in Africa *prior* to slavery.

What were our ancestors really like? What did they do? How did they go about their lives? What did their days look like? Their families? How did they celebrate their culture?

Slavery is a raw topic, full of horror stories, so we also spend months talking about African lives preslavery, as well as celebrating all the creative and wonderful things their ancestors did, the scientists and the inventors.

Reading books with my children starts me on a journey to knowing my own history, where my ancestors are from and what's happened throughout the centuries.

Now I've come to love history.

My history.

I homeschool my children until the end of elementary school, and then we put them in public middle school in St. Louis.

When my twin girls enter the seventh grade, there isn't a single book about Black characters or by a Black author on their reading list.

"I can help you with a list of books, if you'd like, along with descriptions," I tell the superintendent.

The woman is very sweet and kind but says there's nothing she can do. "Unfortunately," she tells me, "all the books for the upcoming school year have already been chosen."

At home, I keep supplementing my kids' learning, creating games and feeding them the cultural food—and biographies—that they need. They're avid readers but don't love reading nonfiction, so our deal is five fiction books to every biography.

It's hard to find the books we want in their school library. We're in a predominantly white area, and the librarian has to request them from other libraries, which takes time.

"Where did you get that book?" their friends start to ask.

"How do your children know so much history?" other parents question.

"Where can I find these books for my classroom?" some teachers ask me.

I'm happy to pass along the names of books and authors. And then I say to my husband, "Hey, why don't we open a bookstore?"

We find a 750-square-foot space. It's tiny, and perfect. We call it EyeSeeMe African American Children's Bookstore, and open on Juneteenth in 2015.

The two of us rush into things blindly. We don't have a business plan. We just see a need in the community.

We don't know anything about the book business. Like,

nothing at all. I have no idea what I'm getting myself into. I don't even know what basic industry terms mean, or how to decide what titles to select, how many copies to stock, et cetera. I simply buy books that I think are interesting. I stock the store with about a hundred titles, from baby board books up to high-school-level reads.

Opening week, we make $50.

The next six months are a tough learning curve. We didn't go into this business to make money, but we *do* have to make enough to cover rent and other expenses.

A teacher gives us our first big sale. "We were just having a conversation in my school about representation, and having more diverse books in our library," she tells me. "Your store is perfect."

There are so many new children's books coming out, so many more Black authors telling stories for Black kids and young adults these days. Sci-fi is very popular, especially futuristic stuff. There are quite a few books for Black girls, but it's harder to find books for Black boys. That can still be a struggle.

I also begin to expand my selection of titles to include books about other people of color, such as Latin and Asian stories. Those books, too, are very rare in the classroom.

I live and breathe the bookstore. There's nothing else that I think about. I'm constantly researching and writing down titles. I want to be able to recommend specific books or make sure we're stocking the books we need. When someone wants, say, a potty-training book featuring toddlers of color, or when a white grandmother comes into the store and asks, "Do you have a book that features a Black grandfather, a white grandma, and a white mom?" I want to be able to give them options.

I get a phone call from a preschool teacher who recently bought a lot of books for her classroom. "I want to share a story with you about a book you recommended."

"Which one?"

"*I'm New Here* by Anne Sibley O'Brien."

This children's book tells the story of three immigrant children—from Guatemala, Korea, and Somalia—who struggle to adapt to their new American schools.

"I have a student from the Middle East," the teacher says. "She's very shy and doesn't speak much. But when I read *I'm New Here* to the class, this little girl just lit up for the first time. After I finished reading it, she came and asked if she could take the book home with her."

The girl took the book home and showed her parents, who were so moved they called the school to express their gratitude. Reading the book in class had such a positive impact on their daughter and her new life here in America.

"It's the first time this little girl actually saw herself in a book," the teacher says. "It makes me so happy to see how this one book has made such a difference in her life. She's participating more in school now, and she's coming out of her shell. Thank you for everything you and your husband are doing to help all the children in our community."

Sarah Galvin

Sarah Galvin and her husband are the owners of
the Bookstore Plus in Lake Placid, New York.

As a kid, I live underneath a bookstore owned by my parents.

It's ironic that I hate reading and want nothing to do with books.

I love learning, and I love being taught, but school is hard for me. Homework assignments that take others half an hour take me three hours. The school can't find the appropriate label for what's wrong with me, so I never receive any special treatment beyond teachers allowing me extra time on tests.

My freshman year of college, I decide to step outside of my comfort zone and take a class called Women and Science Fiction. We're assigned *Parable of the Sower* by Octavia Butler.

Something just clicks. That's when I fall in love with books.

When I'm a junior, my mom comes to me. "One of our employees wants to buy the bookstore," she tells me. "I told her, 'Well, Sarah's an only child. It's her decision if she wants to buy it or not.' I know this is early, and your dad and I aren't pressuring you by any means—"

"She can't buy it. It's mine," I say, surprised by the intensity of my emotions.

So I become a second-generation owner.

A five-year-old boy comes to the counter super excited. He's holding a picture book about beavers. I need to scan the barcode, but he doesn't want to give me the book.

"I don't wanna lose my page," he says.

"I'll put a bookmark in it for you."

"What's a bookmark?"

I put the decorative paper rectangle in his book. "Now you can open right back to your page." His mind is blown.

A mother comes in with her teenage daughter, who heads straight for our section of graphic novels. With everyone so deeply plugged into their phones, it's great to see young adults wanting to find—and connect to—a book.

"All she wants to read are graphic novels," the mother complains. "She's not reading, you know, *real* books."

"If she loves graphic novels, let her read graphic novels," I say. "I didn't pick up a book until I was nineteen."

The mother stares at me, shocked. I know what she's thinking. *How could someone who didn't read until they were nineteen own a bookstore?*

"If she wants to read a magazine, let her read a magazine. If she wants to read *The Guinness Book of World Records,* then let her read that. Don't squash her love of reading. There's so much pressure. Eventually, she'll find books she'll connect with. Just keep reading fun."

During COVID, when we're doing whatever we can to survive, people call over FaceTime and we walk them around the store. A man places an order for a Moleskine journal, and when I call to let him know his order's arrived, he says, "Oh, that's wonderful. Now I have a big favor to ask."

"Okay," I say, wondering what the favor might be.

"I'm here from New York City and we've rented a house and there's no printer. And there's no other place that I can get my last will and testament printed. Will you print that for me?"

"Yeah, absolutely," I tell him. "I'll print it out and have it with your Moleskine when you pick it up."

When he comes to get his order, he asks, "Now, will you be a witness for me?"

"Yes," I answer. "I will certainly be the witness on your will."

Talk about being a full-service bookstore.

I run the bookstore with my husband, Marc. When we have our daughter, I read to her every chance I get. She's the opposite of me as a kid—she *loves* books. Anytime she gets upset, she runs to her room, grabs a book, and we snuggle on the couch together. I feel like I'm making up for lost time, reading the children's books I never read as a kid. We even name our dog Fern after the main character in *Charlotte's Web*.

When people ask, my husband and I say we have one kid and one business—which is a living, breathing entity with multiple identities. I realize it sounds kind of dorky, but it takes me by surprise to learn how much personality a business and a building can have. But now, it's like the bookstore is its own being.

The village of Lake Placid is tiny, maybe 2,800 year-round residents, 5,200 in the greater area. We get a lot of summer tourists, but we really know our locals well. And their support is everything.

One of the high school teachers made a point of consistently going to the school board and saying, "There is no reason we should be shopping with Amazon and getting our books from Amazon. We need to be ordering from the local bookstore."

Now it's just second nature for them to send us their purchase orders.

The business ebbs and flows. We know that our busy eight weeks of summer will carry us to the holidays, which will then carry us back to spring. Our staff is me and Marc, plus a mix of full-timers and part-timers, high schoolers and semiretirees.

One of our older part-timers retired at the end of 2021. But the next year, she calls me and asks, "Will you hire me back? I need to be around people. I miss it. And there's no job I want except to work at the Bookstore Plus."

Kathleen Johnson

Kathleen Johnson is the events coordinator for
Prairie Lights in Iowa City, Iowa.

People who work at bookstores, I find, come in two varieties. The first type is all about the books. They're excited to look through ARCs, curious to hear what other people are reading, and love matching customers with books they'll enjoy. They're interested in what's going on and which authors are coming to read, and—even if they don't love every moment of moving furniture or peeling stickers off unsold books heading to returns—this world makes sense to them.

The second type is smart and agreeable and pleasant in the time they spend working here but are marking time until they can return to their "real" lives. It's not that they aren't helpful and reliable. They just aren't lifers.

I'm definitely in the first category. When I'm in the bookstore,

I'm 100 percent here, and fully committed. Hearing myself say that makes me cringe at how nerdy I sound, but while I certainly don't love every aspect of my job every day, it's always interesting. Though I can also understand the second category, the people who say, "I don't have the energy to interact with anyone. I want to go home, feed my cat, and read my own book."

I get it. Like many readers, I've always been an introvert.

Growing up, I read everything in my grade school library except the Sweet Valley High series, which I wasn't allowed to read—and, truth be told, I didn't have much in common with the Sweet Valley High twins. I wasn't into dating or even hanging out with friends. I just wanted to stay home and read.

My mom was concerned. She once overhead me on the phone turning down a friend who'd asked if I wanted to come over.

"Sorry," I'd said. "I can't today."

When I got off the phone, my mother said, "All you want to do is keep your nose in a book. You need to do something with your friends, or they'll stop inviting you."

I go to college at the University of Iowa because the school has a great English program, and after graduation I stay in Iowa City at my first real "grown-up job" for six years—which is a *long* time when you're in your twenties. I work in human resources, hiring temporary staff, writing the weekly newsletter, and planning the annual corporate family picnic. But I don't have a family, and I don't particularly like picnics. It was a recipe for major depression.

Or maybe a minor existential crisis.

So I quit.

I have a lot of unused vacation time, which gives me a bit of a financial cushion. Time to think about what to do next.

And time to read. I spend a long time just reading books.

When I discover that Prairie Lights, our prestigious local bookstore, is looking to hire a bookseller, it feels right. My old job never made sense to me. Why do people "work"? What is it for? But working in a bookstore—that makes sense.

I start out as a cashier and a "basic" bookseller, helping to sticker and shelve new books. Prairie Lights has a huge inventory. We will often sell more than a thousand different titles a week, which is unusual for a bookstore. Not a thousand books—a thousand unique titles. It's a reflection of the wide-ranging interests of our literary community. Our inventory is completely shaped by what the people of Iowa City like to read.

I'm put in charge of a few different sections, and I do a little bit of everything, along with another new hire, Curtis Sittenfeld, who works part-time because she's also in the University of Iowa's esteemed Writers' Workshop. The Writers' Workshop has produced an astounding number of award-winning authors, journalists, poets, and playwrights. A few years later, Curtis publishes her debut novel, *Prep,* which becomes an acclaimed bestseller.

Over the years, it's been amazing to see so many former university students and faculty return as published authors. I love introducing these authors when they come back to read. It's really magical to have the opportunity to welcome them to the front of the room, have them step up to the microphone at the old dictionary stand we use as a lectern for the readings, and tell the crowd how they too have sat in the green-and-white plastic stacking lawn chairs we always put out for the audience.

I'm shocked at first that my coworkers don't all stick around for every author event we host, but Iowa City is full of writers. I guess there's such a thing as "author fatigue" when you live in a place like this.

I've gotten to know a lot of writers in this job. Many of them come in to spend time at our bookstore café. Some authors intimidate me just by being so sharp and funny; others I worry about, and I want to drag them out of their studies to make sure they're doing all right. It's not uncommon to be neighbors with a *New York Times* bestselling author or to go to the same church as a Pulitzer Prize winner. And in Iowa City, maybe more than in any other city in the country, being a writer is seen as important.

What I truly like best about my job is just being part of the book community, including booksellers, authors, publicists, sales reps, editors, and others. I've never felt more at home with any other group of people. We're a mix of individuals who somehow fit right in with one another—covered in cat hair, wearing Clarks shoes, all of us laughing at the same jokes.

Martha Hickson

Martha Hickson is a librarian for a high school in New Jersey.

I love being a high school librarian. I love how things change every year when the kids come to school. The environment becomes electric. Alive. It keeps me young.

The decision to go to library school comes in my forties, after a career spent working in corporate public relations for AT&T. Lucrative, but not personally satisfying.

The timing works out perfectly—the company is going through layoffs, and my severance package includes a tuition allotment that will cover my first semester. Then, on my first day at library school, I learn that if I enroll in New Jersey's Department of Labor and Workforce Development Program, the state will waive the rest of my tuition at Rutgers for the next two years. I can't believe my good fortune, how everything just effortlessly falls into place.

I end up working in a high school. Teenagers are just puppies with longer legs. They do the goofiest, funniest things, and tell me all kinds of stuff about their lives, hopes, dreams, fears, and insecurities.

Sometimes parents complain about a book in our library. I'll listen to their concerns and then explain the merits of the book in question, why it's in the library collection, and then remind the parent that library books are voluntary reading.

"If the book isn't a good fit for you or your child, they don't have to read it," I tell them. "Just bring the book back."

That conversation usually ends the matter.

In January 2019, a colleague tells me she has been sent by the principal to have me remove a book from the library.

"Which one?" I ask.

"*Fun Home: A Family Tragicomic* by Alison Bechdel."

Cartoonist Bechdel's award-winning graphic memoir—adapted into a Tony Award–winning Broadway musical—recounts her growing up as the gay daughter of a closeted gay father.

"A parent lodged a complaint," my colleague says.

I'm confused. "That's not the process for objecting to a book," I say. "We have a reconsideration process to follow. I won't do it."

Something about this request feels off. I decide to investigate.

No parent lodged the complaint, I discover. It's our own school superintendent and principal who want the book removed.

I stand firm.

"We have a policy in place for challenging books," I tell them. "If you want *Fun Home* removed, you need to follow that policy, which is to file a written complaint. After that, a reconsideration committee will be formed."

Both the principal and the superintendent tell me the policy doesn't apply to them.

"Yes, it does—it must," I explain. "Otherwise, you'd be able to wander freely through the library and cherry-pick any book that offends you."

They still don't get it. It leads to a long, protracted battle that goes on for another eight months. *Fun Home* remains on the shelf.

But I know this isn't over.

On Tuesday, September 28, 2021, I'm eating lunch at my desk and reading the *New York Times Book Review* when the school principal comes into my office. He seems nervous.

"Martha," he says, "I've heard a rumor that there's going to be a book complaint at tonight's board meeting."

"Which book?"

"Gender Queer."

Like *Fun Home*, *Gender Queer* is a graphic memoir about

puberty, gender, and sexuality. It's by Maia Kobabe, a non-binary illustrator. Frank and honest, the book is one of the most challenged in the country.

It's also won prestigious awards. I explain this to the principal as I pull up all the wonderful reviews of the book and print them out for him.

I hand him copies of our selection policy, our reconsideration policy, and the form for requesting reconsideration of a book.

"Having a complaint at a board meeting," I remind him, "is not the way we request reconsideration of a book. We follow policy. You can give the complainant these materials."

At seven that evening, instead of watching *Jeopardy!* as usual with my husband, we tune in to the school board meeting being livestreamed on TV.

The first person to get up and speak is a student.

"Politics, religion, and social issues have no place in a school," he says. "Children should not be educated about those matters."

He takes his seat. A parent, a woman named Gina, is the next speaker.

She launches into a tirade about two books. One is *Gender Queer*. The other is *Lawn Boy* by Jonathan Evison, a coming-of-age novel about a young Mexican American man grappling with racism and class inequality. Gina claims that the books are pornography and then reads various passages taken out of context.

"My sixteen-year-old son was able to check them out," she says. "Martha Hickson, our school librarian, remarked to my son, 'I love that book.'

"This amounts to an effort to groom our kids," she says. "Sex offenders have no place in or even near our schools. Those responsible for this disgusting material in our schools should be required to step down, investigated, and charged accordingly."

I gasp and sit up in my gray recliner.

My heart is racing. My stomach is churning, and I'm physically shaking, my nerves are so on edge. I grab my cell phone and begin typing out and submitting online challenge reports to the American Library Association Office for Intellectual Freedom, the National Coalition Against Censorship, the Comic Book Legal Defense Fund, and the National Council of Teachers of English. I also email my union.

"This is ridiculous," I say to my husband, trying to calm myself. "I hope the administration is going to do something about this."

Three days pass. No one in the school administration speaks to me in any official capacity. On Friday, I finally run into the school principal in the hallway and have a chance to talk to him. "I need to speak with you," I say. "Will there be a statement from the district to support me?"

"Why would we do that?"

I'm so stunned by his question that it takes me a moment to recover. I've dedicated seventeen years to my job. My performance is nothing less than distinguished. I've won national awards for my library work. "I was falsely accused of being a sex offender."

He shrugs. "People are allowed to say whatever they want."

During the next couple of weeks, "Requests for Reconsideration" are submitted for *Gender Queer* and *Lawn Boy,* along with three more books: *All Boys Aren't Blue* by George M. Johnson, *This Book Is Gay* by Juno Dawson, and *Fun Home* (again!) by Alison Bechdel. Emails from certain school parents start targeting me; meanwhile, some students are intentionally hiding library books having to do with homosexuality or gender identity.

The group targeting me is small, but loud and nasty. These parents, I discover, are following the same playbook used by extreme right-wing groups like Moms for Liberty and No Left Turn in Education. The book complaints and manufactured outrage at board meetings are all scripted; they're all told to attack the same books at school libraries across the country.

The stress leads me to go on medical leave and I'm unable to attend the October board meeting. The next morning, I watch the rebroadcast. Nearly 400 community members, including students, stood up for the right to read.

It's beautiful.

The same thing happens at the November board meeting.

In January, the Reconsideration Committee that had been formed back in October to review the five books in question makes its decision: they recommend retaining four of the five books and banning one, *This Book Is Gay*. The board will vote on it on January 25.

I get an idea. The introduction to Juno Dawson's book was written by David Levithan, who is both a wildly popular young adult author and an editor at Scholastic.

I need to get in touch with him.

I reach out to my library network, explaining the situation at my school and asking for Levithan's contact information, and within two hours he and I are emailing back and forth. He agrees to write a letter for a student to read aloud at the school board meeting.

Now it's time for the vote: Three board members abstain. Two vote to ban.

The other seven say, "We're keeping this book."

I weep with relief. An enormous weight has been lifted off my shoulders. But not once during this long ordeal has anyone on the board or in the administration refuted the claims made against me.

Finally, at the February board meeting, the board president reads a letter stating that the claims against me were unfounded.

Unfounded. It's taken me five months to get those three syllables out of the board. It's better than nothing, but not by much.

I'm sixty-two years old. My plan was to retire when I turned sixty-five. If I leave now, my retirement income, which isn't that great to begin with, will be diminished monthly for as long as I live.

I can afford to quit my job, but just barely. "Medicare doesn't kick in until you're sixty-five," my financial planner says. "If you pull the plug now, you'll have to pay for health insurance, which, as I'm sure you already know, can be expensive."

Beyond the costs—significant though they are—if I quit now, I know it will irk me every month when I see that retirement check deposited in my bank account. I know that I will look at that money and think, *I let them do this to me*.

I'm not going to let these sons of bitches pick my pocket in retirement.

I keep thinking about the people who attacked not only me but the books. They say it was for the First Amendment. Well, I'm here for the First Amendment too. We have that in common.

They also say they did it to protect children. We've got that in common too. I'm all about protecting children—and their right to information. If we can have a conversation and not a screaming match around those two fundamental principles, there may be hope.

But my true hope rests with the kids themselves. Those kids who rose up en masse to oppose the efforts to keep them from reading. Those kids who engaged in the civic process and comported themselves beautifully in public discourse. Those kids who are going to be voting sooner rather than later—and the more of them who do that, the better off we'll all be.

Charlene Stoyles

Charlene Stoyles is the customer operations leader at Chapters St. John's, part of the Indigo chain of bookstores, in St. John's, Newfoundland, Canada.

I'm waiting for my lunch at Thai Express when I recognize a woman and her six-year-old daughter in line behind me as regular customers at the bookstore.

The little girl waves, recognizing me too.

The three of us end up sitting at opposite ends of the same long table…but before I know it, the little girl moves down to the seat right next to mine so that she can talk to me about books.

Since books are my favorite thing in the world, I couldn't be more thrilled.

I've been at the store for ten years now. It's my happy place.

I work with an amazing group of people. I couldn't ask for a better group of people to spend my time with.

Before working here, I had no idea how much of this job meant acting as unofficial therapist for customers. Although most people come in just looking to pick up a book for themselves or as a gift, occasionally I'll get a customer looking for something a little deeper. People who need books to help explain death and grief to their children. People looking for books to help them break free of abusive relationships or alcoholism. People looking for guidance as they struggle with wedding planning or child raising. People looking for affirming LGBTQIA+ reads as they come to terms with their sexuality. Or even just lonely people looking for someone to talk to. We handle it all and try to make everyone's day just a little better.

Including our own.

Even though St. John's is the provincial capital here on the island of Newfoundland, it's still a relatively small city, but big enough to support our store as well as two smaller bookstores.

And Newfoundlanders *love* to support their own—as far as I know, we have the largest local interest section in the whole country. We have a lot of book launches for local authors, and we frequently have local authors in for signings. If someone's book is in the local paper or the local news, look out. We won't be able to keep those books on the shelves. Everyone will need a copy.

"Can you make out this last one to me?" I ask Perry Chafe, a Canadian TV writer and producer on the hit shows *Republic of Doyle* and *Son of a Critch*. Chafe lives here on the island, and he's stopped by to sign copies of his debut novel, *Closer by Sea*. I've requested an advance reading copy from the publisher but it hasn't come in. "I promise I'll buy it on my lunch break!" I tell him. I'm happy to support him.

I gather up all the copies of the book we have in stock for him to sign—not nearly enough!—and he's a true pleasure to deal with, open and friendly.

"I'll sign this book for you, Charlene," Chafe tells me, "but only if you let me buy it for you."

Chafe won't take no for an answer. He signs the book and hands it to the cashier.

What a sweet man.

Dale, a regular, comes in looking for a Christmas gift for his wife.

"We have a beautiful, autographed box set of Ken Follett's Century trilogy," I tell him. "I definitely recommend that you buy it for her before I buy it for myself!"

I'm only half-joking—I already own all the Follett books, but the temptation to purchase this signed box set anyway is strong.

Dale is convinced, and the gift is a big hit with his wife, Rita. So much so, he comes back to me again and again for more book recommendations. Eventually, Rita starts coming to me herself, looking for recommendations for her husband. Then their two teenagers start coming to find me. Then Rita's mother. One day, as I'm walking out after my shift, I see the two teens and their grandmother coming in the door—so I turn right back into the store to help them pick out the perfect gift for Dale.

I develop a great relationship with the entire family. They're all still some of my absolute favorite people.

One year around Christmastime, Rita comes to the cash register where I'm working.

"Have you read this one yet?" she asks as I'm ringing up her purchase, a copy of *The Night Circus* by Erin Morgenstern.

"I haven't had the chance," I admit, "but I've heard great things about it."

"Perfect," she says. "This is for you. After all the great books you've recommended to us over the years, this one is my recommendation to you."

I'm incredibly touched.

I love interacting with customers. Just being a small part of their lives and knowing that I have given them the gift of books means the world to me.

Bill Kelly

Bill Kelly is the adult programming manager for the Cuyahoga County Public Library in Northeast Ohio, near Cleveland.

I enter the library and see a job listing tacked to the corkboard in the lobby.

The library is looking for an assistant. I read the qualifications.

Must enjoy reading and enjoy reference and helping people locate the materials they need, whether it's for research papers, homework, job searches, etc.

It's like I'm reading my own biography.

I'm an avid, wide-ranging reader, a few years out of college with a degree in literature and philosophy.

I've spent a lot of time in libraries—"Palaces for the People," according to industrialist Andrew Carnegie, who donated

$60 million of the fortune he'd made in steel to build nearly 2,000 libraries. But I've never considered working in one.

The idea of helping people fulfill their curiosities is very appealing and lines up with my lifelong passion for "intellectual history," books about how ideas have evolved over the course of centuries and inspired people to have even more ideas.

I should probably apply for this job, I think. *Something tells me I'm exactly who they're looking for.*

I do, and I am. I get the job.

My first night, I'm working the reference desk when an older gentleman comes up and tells me, "I want to start a lapidary hobby."

I try to recall what *lapidary* means. It makes me realize the scope of my ignorance. Like so many people, I live in my own little world.

"Gemstones," he explains. "I need books about working with gemstones, how to polish them, engrave them, et cetera."

I take him over to the stacks, then I sit examining books with him, making sure they'll be useful. I know next to nothing about gemstones, but I'm a lifelong learner. This job helps me expand my knowledge and also expands my world—it's so fascinating to accompany people, like this gentleman, at the start of their journeys.

It feels like a special gift to be allowed to tag along and hang out with people exploring their own curiosity or hobbies, passions, interests. I have no idea what I might learn on any given day.

Ohio loves its libraries. Cuyahoga County Public Library has been named the number one library system in the country for twelve straight years in the same category as the New York public libraries and the Boston public libraries. We serve forty-seven communities with twenty-seven branches.

I oversee all of the library's adult programs, for anyone eighteen and over. We do a lot of job training. We have a writers center. We started a culinary literacy program: mobile kitchens where we teach how to prepare a nutritional meal at an affordable cost. The library is really positioned to be the center of community life.

Author events are my favorite. We try to have something for everyone. Literary authors, debut authors, nonfiction, every genre. I love nothing more than seeing people in the signing line, talking to authors. There's a special connection.

One of my most memorable events is with Margaret Atwood, right after the TV adaptation of her novel *The Handmaid's Tale* wins eight Emmy Awards in its first season. I interview her onstage, and she's so charming and witty. We have a great talk.

Afterward, one of the attendees comes up and says, "Wow, did you guys plan that? You two were like a comedy team."

What really sticks with me is her attitude that when you

read a book, it's only half the conversation. You yourself are the other half of that conversation. We all bring our own history, our own psychology, even our own subconscious, to every book we read. So in a way, we're all reading a different book.

Libraries level the playing field. They're free and open to the public. All are welcome. Our doors are open. Come in and learn to become your best self. Follow your dreams and reach your true potential. Let your reach exceed your grasp. Whatever book you want to read, it's free on the honor system.

It's hard to imagine anywhere else in our society so devoted to the concept of everyone being completely equal.

Janice Turbeville

Janice Turbeville works for Barnes & Noble in Seattle, Washington. She was formerly the store manager and is currently a project manager with the store planning and design team.

J anice," my mom says wearily, "it's dinnertime. Please put the book down so you can eat and talk to me and your father about your day."

I'm an only child. I don't have any siblings to play with, so I always have a book, even at family get-togethers and parties.

My absolute favorite book is *The True Confessions of Charlotte Doyle* by Avi. In the summer of 1832, thirteen-year-old schoolgirl Charlotte Doyle is the only passenger on a transatlantic journey from Liverpool, England, to Providence, Rhode Island, when the ship's crew mutinies, and Charlotte must decide whether to side with the captain or the rebellious crew.

I read it till the cover comes off, and then I buy another copy.

I love reading. And book clubs. The first one I joined was the American Girl Book Club, hosted by my local Barnes & Noble in Golden, Colorado. When I aged out of that book club, I moved into one for fourth and fifth graders.

One day, the store's community relations manager comes up to me and says, "Would you like to run the book club?"

I'm thrilled. "Yeah, totally."

My friend and I run the club as volunteers. When we turn sixteen, the store asks if we'd like to do some part-time work.

"Absolutely!"

I'm hired to dress up as costumed characters for their monthly story times—the bunny from *Goodnight Moon* or a character from *Love You Forever,* whatever the store needs. I work for the store until I graduate from high school.

In college, I work for a Barnes & Noble in Bellingham, Washington. By the time I graduate, I've been promoted to the management team. The store offers me a full-time job.

I've now been working for Barnes & Nobles for nearly twenty years. It's literally the only job I've ever had.

I'm often asked why I've stayed in the business for so long, and my answer is that it's the people. It's such a cliché answer, but it's the truth. I'm not exaggerating when I say the best people in my life are all folks from Barnes & Noble. I met my husband through Barnes & Noble, I met my best friend working here—it is just by far the best group of people I have ever known.

TikTok has really changed the business for middle grade and teenage books. Any book that kids are reading these days, I swear it's something they've found through social media.

Honestly, it's been kind of mind-blowing. It's so cool to see kids making such a strong connection with books at a fairly young age.

Manga—the genre of comics and graphic novels from Japan—is very popular with teenagers and twentysomethings. It's one of our top-selling categories, and I'm willing to bet that's true in almost every Barnes & Noble across the country. Never in a million years would I have thought manga could outsell fiction, but it can and does.

Our store is on the north side of the city and right on a light-rail track, one of Seattle's public transit options. We get a lot of foot traffic—and a lot of colorful, eclectic characters, like Nerf Guy. His real name, I think, is Josh, and every time he comes into the store, he's carrying anywhere between three and thirteen Nerf guns.

And sometimes a lightsaber.

We get a lot of browsers, but also people just coming in to use the bathroom—or shoplift.

Surprisingly, books aren't the primary target, although I recently did witness a guy grab three Stuart Woods and three John Grisham paperbacks off the shelf and stick them in his pockets.

"Hey, I need those back," I tell him.

He says nothing, walks right past me and out the door, and then he takes off running.

He says nothing, walks right past me and out the door, and then he takes off running.

"Excuse me," says a voice behind me.

I turn and see an older gentleman. He gives me a sheepish expression and says, "I have a weird request."

Uh-oh, I think, forcing a smile.

"I really like doing puzzles," he says.

So far, so good. A lot of people love puzzles. They flew off the shelves during COVID. We were closed but allowed to deliver items for curbside pickup, and nine out of ten items we delivered were puzzles.

Never in my wildest dreams did I ever think we'd sell so many puzzles; but I also never expected a pandemic.

"What I'd like," the older man says, "is for you to pick the puzzle for me."

"Sure, I can do that."

"Here's my credit card. Could you please pick out a couple of puzzles for me, but don't tell me what they are? After you ring them up, would you mind opening the boxes and putting each set of the puzzle pieces in a plastic bag?" The sheepish look returns.

"Like I said, I know it's a weird request, but I don't want to know the final picture ahead of time. It's one of the brain exercises I do to keep my mind sharp."

"That's awesome." I laugh. "Yes, I can absolutely do that for you—would *love* to do it for you."

I mean it. I love quirky requests.

If you come into my store and say, "I need a book about technological advancements during the 1920s," I'll marshal all my resources to help you find the perfect book that you can't wait to get home and read.

Books have deep connections. People are always looking for books on big life events—relationships, breakups, deaths, grief, getting married or what to expect when you're pregnant—and there's nothing better than recommending books that can have a meaningful and positive impact on someone's life.

Sarah Hobbs

Sarah Hobbs is the customer experience representative at Indigo Books in Brampton, Ontario, Canada.

Most books publish on Tuesdays, and that's when customers come in for new releases.

About twenty years ago, in the days before online ordering, one of my favorite customers, Linda, would call every Tuesday, like clockwork. We had a routine down: she'd place an order and pay over the phone, then I'd package up her purchases for her to collect by taxi.

Tuesdays are still my favorite days—I love seeing people excited for their preorders and what's hot off the press!—but there is so much to love about every day in the store.

I love the special feeling that comes when I make a connection with patrons. I cannot help but feel emotionally attached to the people who come in: the repeat customers who remember you and want more recommendations, the people enduring some of the worst days of their lives, the ones celebrating their happiest events.

I love every second of the job, but being a bookseller is very hard work. Not only physically but mentally too. I have to be able to locate stock, give recommendations on the fly, and juggle multiple customers simultaneously. I rely on technology, but it sometimes fails—which is when my years of experience really kick in, and I pull up every bit of information buried deep in the recesses of my memory.

That's when I'm especially grateful for customers like Linda. The two of us always have a nice chat, especially because we are both book lovers and are both originally from the UK.

There's something so special about sharing the experience of a book. My favorite genres are mystery and historical fiction, though I also like the occasional nonfiction book—and recently I've started reading romance too. I work in all the areas of my store, so I try to be flexible.

My career began in my student days when I worked Saturdays as a librarian's assistant at our local branch. Then I got hired in both the books and entertainment departments at WHSmith, a UK retailer since 1792. "Keep the customer at the heart of all that we do" is their company motto, one I've made my own.

Twenty-four years ago, I married my husband and moved from the UK to Toronto, Canada.

"I hear there's a bookstore opening in the neighborhood,"

my husband tells me as soon as we settle into our new home. "You should apply as soon as you can!"

I do, and six weeks later I'm working at Chapters Runnymede.

I've now worked in three different Chapters/Indigo locations, and each store is unique.

Chapters Runnymede was a real neighborhood store, with an architectural history dating back to the 1920s as a vaudeville theater and the 1930s as a cinema. Chapters converted it to a bookstore in 1999 but kept it structurally intact, as it's designated a heritage building. Alas, these days it's no longer in use as a bookstore—it's now a beautiful drugstore.

Indigo Yorkdale is in a mall and serves a much more transient customer base. Lots of people passing through or just visiting the mall for the day.

Indigo Brampton, where I am now, is again much more of a neighborhood store that's truly a part of our customers' lives. We see couples marry and have babies, and children turn into teenagers. The local dogs all love visiting to get petted and fawned over by the staff!

What's even more fun is when a teenager comes up to the cash register with a book I'm reading—I adore kids' books and YA—and we can chat about it. It's really lovely to see teens coming in and buying recommended books by the handful, and then a few weeks later coming in for more. They swap them with friends and share a newfound love of reading. There are teens buying manga who never wanted to read before but are now hooked.

TikTok has definitely helped physical book sales in the last few years. Social media is winning in this regard.

As a bookseller, I have the privilege of hosting many authors and also attending many book launches and meet and greets. Every event and book launch is special—but one leaves me speechless.

It's for Chris Hadfield, the Canadian astronaut and former commander of the International Space Station, and the author of *An Astronaut's Guide to Life on Earth,* as well as the Apollo Murders thriller series, among other titles.

Despite having been to so many other book launches— including for some of my favorite UK authors, like Clare Mackintosh, Peter James, Stuart MacBride, Jojo Moyes, and Lisa Jewell—this one just leaves me in awe.

As the real-life astronaut shakes my hand, it's like an out-of-body experience for me. All intelligent thought leaves my head.

"Hi!" is all I manage to squeak out before the moment is over. Thank goodness for the photos—and my treasured signed copy.

Bob Wells

*Bob Wells is the founder and former owner of
the Rainbow News and Café in Winston-Salem,
North Carolina.*

I decide to open a newsstand on Main Street in Winston-Salem. I rent space in an old building downtown, hire some contractors to refurbish the interior.

A friend and I stand on the sidewalk, observing the work in progress. "I still haven't come up with a name for this place," I say. "You have any ideas?"

While my friend thinks, one of the painters turns around and says, "Why don't you call it Rainbow Newsstand?"

I like it. "Okay," I say. "That's what we'll do."

It's the late 1970s, and Winston-Salem has recently gotten an influx of folks moving down here from the North, looking for the *New York Times* and the *Washington Post,* which aren't distributed down here. I see a market, and I get the papers flown down every morning. We take off pretty well.

As we grow, I add a little café area, and change the name to Rainbow News and Café. To decorate the café area, I order a specially made neon sign that says RAINBOW NEWS AND CAFÉ to attract customers. It was the most expensive sign I ever had in my life. It was always burning out.

Then I start thinking, *Why don't I add books? I know a lot about books. I love books. I know people around here would love books.*

They do.

Before long, I decide to expand. I purchase three Victorian homes and combine them into one big, funky, warm, comfortable, and safe place for book lovers. We build a reputation for carrying a wide assortment of books, including hard-to-find titles. I also expand the café into a restaurant that serves sit-down meals. Next door, I open a used-book store, Again & Again, which my sister Janet runs.

Rainbow News and Café becomes a Winston-Salem destination, a place to go. The University of North Carolina School of the Arts is nearby on South Main, and there's a film school, so it's not unusual to see movie and TV people stop by and peruse our shelves. A lot of people come in every day, get coffee, sit down, read books. We do book readings and poetry readings. We host special dinners. People bond over their favorite books and gather to meet new people and to learn about new authors.

It's a really fun place to work. A really gratifying place to work.

Friday nights are big for us. Book browsing followed by dinner out is a double draw that brings people in to walk among the shelves, sit outside on our large Victorian porch.

One Friday night, we're busy as usual—totally full. People are sitting on the porch, drinking coffee and talking about books. Then out of nowhere, rain starts pouring down. Everyone outdoors rushes inside for cover. I look out the windows at a sky bruised grayish purple with the rotational force of ominous-looking black clouds. Within seconds, the rain starts blowing sideways with a kind of power I've never witnessed.

We're all scared to death. It's clear we're in the path of a tornado.

It touches down a couple of blocks from the store. The power goes out and the wind is *howling*. Trees and branches and glass and God only knows what else are being blown around the store. We shelter in place, listening to the wrenching sounds of the porch—moments ago filled with happy customers—being torn to shreds.

When the tornado starts to die down, I pull out bottles of wine and walk the floor, handing out free drinks, trying to get everyone to calm down.

Half an hour later, when it's clear that the tornado is gone, I leave the bookstore through a back door. A pair of massive oak trees have been pulled out of the ground. One of the trees has knocked the chimney off a store building and crushed part of the roof of our restaurant's kitchen.

The other tree has fallen on the back entrance to another

building—and a woman is trapped underneath it, soaking wet and petrified. I run to help, praying for her.

Luckily, one of the oak's branches has wedged into the ground, creating a gap just large enough for me to sneak the woman out from beneath the tree.

I'm so thankful that she isn't badly hurt.

The next morning, I wake up, force myself out of bed.

It's a beautiful sunshiny day, but my thoughts are dark. *How am I going to get this disaster cleaned up? Will I ever be able to get back in business?*

I've got to go down to the store and assess the damage. The roads aren't passable by car, so I walk.

The entire downtown area looks much, much worse in the daylight. Nearly every inch of the street and my property is covered in fallen trees, huge branches, downed power lines, garbage, everything. My buildings have taken a good amount of damage.

I stare at a baby stroller sticking out of the mess.

I stand there, not knowing what to do, not wanting to do anything. But what choice do I have?

Might as well start cleaning up.

I manage to drum up a chain saw. As I get to work sawing branches, I can't escape the feeling of impossible loss that comes with a sinking reality. My business has been destroyed.

I'm sawing through yet another downed tree when a couple approaches. I recognize the woman. She's a frequent customer.

"This is my boyfriend," she says. "We'd love to help you out."

"Sure," I say. "I'd be glad to have you."

They help me clean up.

Before I know it, more of my regular customers have stopped by to help. More than a dozen, maybe twenty or more people, come by. Many of them live in the neighborhood and, even though their own homes are surely damaged, here they are freely giving their time and labor to help me.

One offers to haul the branches away in his pickup truck. Some get to work inside the restaurant cooking up meals for the spontaneous cleaning crew. Others help sort and reshelve the books.

I pause what I'm doing and take in the scene. And I listen as my customers begin to speak my blessings aloud.

One says, "I absolutely adore Rainbow News. It's a home away from home for so many of us."

Another says, "It's such a warm and inviting place. I don't know what I'd do without it."

I'm dumbfounded but grateful. Very grateful. I had no idea so many people value the Rainbow News and Café community this highly. That, like me, they truly enjoy this place of collaboration and exchange.

It isn't just about books. It's social. It's very special to have been a part of a place like that.

Casey Gerken

Casey Gerken is the owner of Innisfree Bookshop in Meredith, New Hampshire.

I want to move to New England so I can be closer to my family.

It's 2008 and we're living in Colorado with our very young daughter. My family lives in Virginia. If we move to the East Coast, travel will be significantly less of a hassle.

So at the end of the year, we pack up and move to Meredith, New Hampshire, a small scenic town near Lake Winnipesaukee.

I have a master's in architecture from Virginia Tech, but I want to spend more time with my daughter. I decide to get a part-time job, something local, with flexible hours.

Innisfree Bookshop, the town's local independent bookstore, is hiring.

I've loved books since I was a kid. My grandmother used to give me books and magazine subscriptions on my birthday, and every year I participated in the library's summer reading program.

And I loved—absolutely *loved*—the Scholastic Book Fair. What kid doesn't get a thrill when receiving that little piece of paper listing all the books you can order?

I get the job and start out as a frontline bookseller. The store's downtown location is bucolic. I can see the water from the store. One of the bookstore's owners is a huge fan of William Butler Yeats and named the bookstore, which opened in 1992, after the Yeats poem "The Lake Isle of Innisfree."

I do a little bit of everything—wholesale buying, inventory. Even though it's the twenty-first century, the store operations are still all done using paper. When an employee rings up a purchase, another employee writes down the titles of all the books people buy. Then it's someone else's job to walk around the store and count how many of those titles we have left, and how many we need to order.

There is no computerized inventory system, just index cards that are stored in so many boxes I've lost count. Still, the store operates like a well-oiled machine.

In 2013, I receive a job offer from an architectural firm in Manchester. Although it's an hour commute each way, my daughter is older now, so I accept their offer and leave the bookstore.

It's a great job. I enjoy the work and my colleagues. I could see myself working there until I retire—but after a few years, the firm is restructured, and my hours are reduced. I'm about to turn fifty and think to myself, *I don't want to go looking for a new job, not at this age. I'd rather do my own thing.*

But I have no idea what that "thing" is.

That changes during a lunch with my old bookstore friends. We chat about what's going on at Innisfree—staffing issues and people retiring. And how the two store owners are getting older.

As we talk, I have a vision of what I could do to update Innisfree. What it would be like to own and run the bookstore.

The more I think about it…the whole thing feels right.

I mull over the idea for a couple of months. My husband encourages me to go for it.

I email my former boss at Innisfree. "What's your exit strategy?" I ask. "What are you and your partner going to do with Innisfree when you decide to retire?"

He sends me back a one-sentence reply.

"This is interesting, we should talk."

Six months later, the bookstore's mine. I take over in the summer of 2017, on the store's twenty-fifth anniversary.

A woman bundled in a winter parka paces back and forth outside the bookstore, waiting for me to unlock the front door.

Her name is Joanne. She's a regular customer.

What I love the most about this job is interacting with customers, but these days I'm not on the sales floor all that much. As the owner, most of my work, sadly, is done sitting behind a computer handling tasks like inventory, title ordering, and preparing for meetings and upcoming conferences. And I'm always trying to keep us connected with other art- and literature-oriented community groups, local theater groups and the like. I go to a lot of board meetings.

In addition to our fantastic year-round customers—who stick with us through thick and thin, popping by to see if we have the latest book they heard about on NPR or from our newsletter—we also have a lot of seasonal visitors. There are a lot of families who for generations have owned lake homes up here, and it's always super fun to reconnect in the summertime. I love it when readers come in with their friends and relatives or the newest members of their families. "Oh my gosh, this is one of my favorite places! We've been coming here forever!" they exclaim. It's a really nice part of what we do; it makes us feel like we're a part of so many families.

I can do bookstore-related work anywhere, anytime, all day long, though the pandemic has forced me to refocus. My husband travels for work and is only home on weekends, so I am trying to learn to "turn it off" and step away a bit. And I'm very lucky that since I have such an amazing staff, I am able to do that.

It's coming up on ten. Time to open.

After a quick hello, Joanne makes a beeline to the new releases table and picks up a hardcover copy of Lee Child's latest Jack Reacher novel, which goes on sale today.

Back in 2011, when Tom Cruise announced he would be

playing Jack Reacher in an upcoming movie, Joanne and my then coworker Kathy—also a huge Jack Reacher fan—were nearly apoplectic.

"No, no, *no*," Kathy said. *"That's not right."*

Joanne nodded in agreement. "Jack Reacher is six feet five inches tall and weighs nearly two hundred and fifty pounds—and it's all muscle. Tom Cruise is nowhere near that!"

The two women never simply discussed the plots or which books were their favorite in the series, or whether the newest book was as good as the previous one. All they talked about was Reacher. They analyzed everything he said and did as though Lee Child's hero was an actual flesh-and-blood human being.

For instance, Joanne would pick up her coffee cup and say, "This is how Reacher drinks his coffee."

"But Reacher would never drink coffee out of a cup like that," Kathy would point out.

Discussions like this have been going on for years in the store—and even in my home. My husband is also a big Jack Reacher fan. He drinks his coffee in what he believes would be a Reacher-approved mug.

One of the other assistant managers, a very pragmatic woman, often got exasperated by their conversation. "You guys," she'd say every time, "you do realize Jack Reacher is *not* a real person."

Kathy and Joanne were undeterred. "Talk to the hand," Joanne told her. "We can't hear you."

Listening to Kathy and Joanne talking about Reacher

reminded me of my second-grade teacher reading us Roald Dahl's *James and the Giant Peach*. I thought it was just the most magical book I'd ever heard. Dahl's characters might be absurd, but I found them very identifiable.

I have to get back to work. Last October, we opened a second Innisfree Bookshop in nearby Laconia, which hasn't had a bookstore in over a decade. I think it's the right time, even though everything I hear on the radio about the current state of the economy is a little frightening.

But I'm doing it anyway. I have a vision.

ABOUT THE AUTHORS

James Patterson is the most popular storyteller of our time. He is the creator of unforgettable characters and series, including Alex Cross, the Women's Murder Club, Jane Effing Smith, and Maximum Ride, and of breathtaking true stories about the Kennedys, John Lennon, and Princess Diana, as well as our military heroes, police officers, and ER nurses. He has co-authored #1 bestselling novels with Bill Clinton and Dolly Parton, told the story of his own life in *James Patterson by James Patterson*, and received an Edgar Award, ten Emmy Awards, the Literarian Award from the National Book Foundation, and the National Humanities Medal.

Matt Eversmann retired from the US Army after twenty years of service. His first book with James Patterson was *Walk in My Combat Boots*.

ABOUT THE AUTHORS

Chris Mooney is the internationally bestselling author of fourteen thrillers. The Mystery Writers of America nominated *Remembering Sarah* for an Edgar Award. He teaches creative writing at Harvard.

For a complete list of books by
JAMES PATTERSON

VISIT
JamesPatterson.com

 Follow James Patterson on Facebook
@JamesPatterson

 Follow James Patterson on X
𝕏 **@JP_Books**

 Follow James Patterson on Instagram
@jamespattersonbooks